RAISE YOUR STANDARDS

STOP EXISTING

START LIVING

Papa Cheikh Diouf

Published by Papadiouf.com

Dedicated
to my
mom

TABLE OF CONTENTS

INTRODUCTION

When you were born, you were crying while the world rejoiced, thinking that someone was coming to save the world. You should live your life in such a way that when you die, the world cries while you rejoice. When Dr Martin Luther King, Steve Jobs, and Michael Jackson died, the world cried so hard because of what they were able to accomplish. If you watch or read their autobiography, you might form an idea that it will be hard to duplicate their success in these times we live in. Matching what Ford, Gandhi, Abraham Lincoln, Dr King, Edison, Tesla, Jobs, and Bezos did would be extremely hard, but it's possible, caused their success left whole lots of clues for me and you to follow if we want to replicate it. They're all self-made, started from nothing and worked their way up to the top.

Let's say you want to replicate their success. Do you think it's possible to accomplish the level of success Apple Founder Steve Jobs had? I have asked the same question to numerous people, and I kept getting the same answer "No. Mr Jobs was a genius." However, Richard B. Fuller said, "

Everyone is born a genius, but the process of living de-geniuses them".

There is nothing impossible. If you break down the word impossible, it means I'M POSSIBLE. You can do anything you put your mind to. If you have a strong desire to succeed, a strong why, you can bear any how.

I immigrated to the USA in 1999 from Senegal, west Africa, and learned English from watching closed captions on TV. I have struggled for a while to find a way to make a living in New York. To get to the top, I have invested countless hours in libraries, reading and researching in the area of human development. I wanted to understand the psychology of success, learn from the best who succeeded at the highest level, the world's best entrepreneurs, and find out what separates them from the pack. I primarily wrote this book for myself as my manual for success.

In this book, I will dissect the myth of success. I will go in depth on how to approach life like the bamboo tree, which doesn't show much growth on the surface in the first five years. However, after the bamboo tree is established, it becomes unstoppable in its growth above the ground, becoming taller and stronger every year. It takes time to learn and to be the best. You just got to trust the process and be extremely patient while you are working hard at it.

Whatever you are trying to do right now, I bet someone has already done it and written a book about it or given a TED talk or made a YouTube video to show you how to do it.

You and I are one decision away from having a totally different life. When you make a decision, that means you cut away all the other options. They say if you want to take over the island, you burn the boat, leaving yourself with no other option but to win. Decision shapes your life. The quality of your life has been the quality of your decisions

Deciding to be successful, believing in yourself, and keeping on trying until it works mindset is key to your success. This book is full of ideas and stories that will help you get whatever you desire. You are the main architect of your life's experience, not the manager of circumstances.

Let's dive into this book.

LIFE IS MEANT TO BE LIVED

Chapter 1

Vision

In April 1999, I got accepted into Pasadena City College, located ten minutes north of Los Angeles. I came to the U.S. that summer but never set foot in that school. The money for school got delayed, and my mom could not pay, which changed everything. To this day, 23 years later, I'm still thinking about what my life would have become if I did attend college there. Instead, I struggled big time in the cold winter of New York City, doing odd jobs, receiving minimum wage, sharing rooms, and sleeping on friends' couches.

I will never forget my first paycheck – it was $240 for one week, working 11 hours per day, 66 hours per week, and one day off. I was working in a retail store owned by a Jewish guy on Gates Avenue in Brooklyn. I was this big security guard, checking people's bags and receipts as they came out of the store. I was shocked when the manager gave me $240 in cash the first week. That was a lot of money in my eyes at that time. Where I'm from, some people don't even get that much money working for the whole month, and I got that in a week! God Bless the U.S.A.! I started to think that if I kept working there for a couple of years, I could own a large chunk of land in Senegal and buy a lovely house for my mom and me. I was the happiest dude in the city. Every day on my way to work, I was elated and grateful for the opportunity – it was fantastic!!!

Yeah, right. That mindset lasted for one week. When I began to buy stuff and ask people how much rent and utilities cost, I realized how much it truly costs to live in New York. Good thing I was staying with a friend of my brother and sleeping on his couch. He was not charging me rent or food; he was looking out for me at that time. After my second week at that job, I was out. I did not even give them a day's notice. The manager was upset that I wanted to leave. He said he would give me a raise right away. A few days before that, he asked me if I knew of other people from Africa looking for a job because if I brought him someone, he would give me more money. Hiring an African American was out of the question. Nobody in their right mind who was born in this country would ever work there. They needed foreigners who just got off the boat, brand new, so they could exploit them before they even knew what was going on.

I quit before I got another job. I was so frustrated that I was being taken advantage of, working 66 hours a week for a lousy $240. I then stumbled through job after job for many years, struggling big time. I had a backpack and a Metro Card. I was all over the five boroughs of New York City.

I started to wonder why people were dying to come to the U.S. For what reason? They say it's easier to make it in the U.S., but I did not believe it. I worked for Domino's, delivering pizza in Manhattan with a bike. I washed pots at Aramark, in school cafeterias, Yankee Stadium, chain restaurants, and Chinese restaurants. I once worked at a temp agency in Manhattan. Some dude named Trevor was the manager. He sent me all over the place in the city and New Jersey. I was working at a Chinese restaurant once. They gave me pots to wash, which were so big, I could have fit into them easily. I was working; it was survival for me. I had no plan or vision; I got up and went to work.

On weekends sometimes, I'd hang out with my friend Badou. We used to go out and meet other Senegalese people who were just as confused as we were. We weren't speaking English like Americans, so people were taking advantage of us easily. I came to realize that we were all doing the same thing, facing challenges in the greatest city in the world, and we did not even have a clue what was going on – no plan, no vision, no direction, no mentors, no advice – learn as you go. Most of us were very disappointed because this was not what we heard or saw on T.V. when we were back in Senegal. New

York City is the concrete jungle, as singer Alicia Keys said. If you can make it here, you can make it anywhere. But how?

Someone told me to get a girlfriend so I could learn how to speak English fast. I took his advice. I was lucky to meet Diane, a very nice white woman who wanted to learn to speak French at that time. She was taking French classes in school, so we were a perfect match – I wanted to learn to speak English, and she wanted to learn French, which is my first language. So, we helped each other. She taught me a whole lot. One day she asked me if I wanted to meet her parents in Wilmington, Delaware, and spend the night at their house. I told her, "You must be out of your mind. I will never do such a thing, like Eddie Murphy in Coming to America." I did not have a problem meeting her parents, but the fact that she asked me to spend the night was out of the question. I was raised in a Muslim country. If my sister had done that, my father would have shot her right then and there (lol). It was tough to get laid in Senegal back then. Girls wouldn't even kiss you. Diane convinced me to go, and we had a good time. I met her parents and spent the night in a separate room.

That was the first time I interacted with a white American family. It was interesting how parents were devoted to seeing their kids prosper. They sit at the dining table, all talking, laughing, and having fun with their parents. I loved that open relationship; it was inspiring to me. I had never seen anything like that. My dad did not have that loving relationship with me. We didn't sit at the same table during lunch or dinner, kids sat with kids, and adults sat with adults. My dad was just there. I couldn't talk to him. Even to this day, I don't have a relationship with my dad, and he's almost 90 years old. I used to call him to check in on him once a week, but our conversation was empty. After I asked how he was doing, nothing was left to discuss. I was not scared of him, but we had no bond. I was just his kid, and he was just my father. That was it.

Diane was teaching me English. Every day I went to the library to watch movies with closed captions. It was like a religion to me. I had to do it every single day. I wanted to learn and understand the language so badly that nothing else mattered. The library was about a two-mile walk. I was covering that distance twice a day. At one point, I stole someone's bike. The bike had just been sitting there for a couple of weeks. Every day I walk by it. I was looking at the bike, and the bike was looking at me. So, one day I decided to "borrow it" because my feet were killing me from the walk. No one ever claimed it, so I kept riding it. I became even more motivated to show up at the library every day. My efforts showed results as my English was getting better and better.

In studying Michael Beckwith's teachings, He said, "pain pushes until vision pulls." Having a strong vision for your life will help you navigate through the pain. We're all in some pain, something we don't want, stress, anxiety, and the only way out of that pain is to have a vision big enough to pull us out. If you don't have a vision, you will remain in that unbreakable cycle, thinking that life is unfair. Growing up in Senegal, West Africa, was painful for millions of people. The pain is still there today because the vision of the so-called leaders is so weak and small to lift the country out of poverty. Maybe they don't have a vision in the first place.

Senegal has had four presidents in 61 years. Still, things have remained almost the same, and the struggle is even more intense today, despite globalization and considerable advances in technology and the internet. Stupid diseases that could be easily cured still kill some people. Where there is no vision, people perish. Someone once said, "An army of sheep led by a lion will always defeat an army of lions led by a sheep." A visionary leader is everything.

Having a vision is crucial to anyone. What got you where you are today won't get you out of it. Your thinking must be bigger than your problems.

Picture yourself sitting at home at your kitchen table with a big juicy lemon on a plate in front of you. Now take a knife and cut the lemon in half. Smell and feel the juice. Now cut a slice from one half. More juice, more smell. Cut that slice in half. More juice, more scent, Cut that slice in half. More juice, more scent, Now take that half, bring it up to your face, take a whiff and then bite into it. If you're like most folks, there is a bit of moisture in your mouth right now. Here's the cool thing. There is no lemon.

Through the power of vision, you have created a physiological response in your body. A vision is the most basic human emotion that you intend to experience in your life. Our brains are incredibly complex; we have the Reticular Activating System (R.A.S.), a bundle of nerves at our brainstem that filters out unnecessary information, so the important stuff gets through. I remember contemplating buying a BMW 7 series; I started to visualize myself behind the wheel of a black BMW 750. Then I went to the dealership to test drive the car, and guess what? I started seeing the same car everywhere; many people were driving the exact vehicle. The R.A.S. realized that the car was important to me now and started to allow more information about it into my consciousness. As a result, I began to see this car everywhere.

When you have a clear vision, your brain helps you to notice whatever can help you bring your vision to reality. The clearer your vision, the quicker your brain will respond and help you. So, get clear and get going. Your vision has to be crystal clear, well-defined and explained in a way that even a five-year-old can understand. It has to be exciting, something you deeply care about, to pull you through when times get tough because it will be challenging, and you will be tested for sure. The road to success is tricky; you've got to be in love with your vision. I can't stress enough how important this is. You don't want to cruise through life to the end only to realize that you did not accomplish anything and that you could have done more than you did.

Once the vision is defined, explained, understood, clarified, established, and all that good stuff, you have got to work to make it happen by setting your short-and long-term goals toward your vision. Without them, it will be just a dream.

I often strike up a conversation with strangers. I asked them about their visions, goals, and what they wanted for their lives. Most of them said they didn't know or had no clue. They want more money – of course, who doesn't want more money? Money is a byproduct. You can't just chase money because you won't catch it; it will always run faster than you. You can't be in business just for the money either – that will make you miserable. You have got to be in tune with what you do and love what you do. That's how you attract money. If you are selling a product or offering a service, find the best way to do it with love and passion. Then the money will take care of itself.

One guy told me that his job doesn't pay him enough, and he's the hardest worker in the company; he should be getting more. Just being the hardest worker in the company doesn't mean you should be getting more money or promoted. It's the value you bring to the marketplace that counts. Stop blaming your employer for not getting the money you want. Oh! The company does not pay; how many people at your job getting paid more than you? The company pays; it's just what they pay you. It makes perfect sense for the company to pay you more if you become more valuable to them. Make yourself more valuable.

I spend time in the morning to visualize my outcome for the day, trying to get myself centered and onboard for the first few minutes of my day by explaining, revisiting, and recreating the vision I have, and that's what keeps me focused. Earl Nightingale said, "You become what you think about." I meditate every morning to calm down and visualize the perfect day. It helps me to navigate through problems and setbacks during the day. I welcome and embrace each one of them. I see them as opportunities to grow cause without them; you can't grow.

A vision of what you truly want will help you create a roadmap to excelling. Saying to yourself, "Oh, I want to stop smoking," or "I want to lose 40 pounds." Those aren't visions; they're not motivating enough. You should say, "My vision is to get back to my perfect weight, to appear sexy, healthy, and beautiful, so I can look at myself in the mirror and not laugh but be proud of myself." That's where losing a few pounds, going to the gym, eating healthy, and getting proper rest, come in, and those are the steps to realizing your vision.

Visualize your life as a successful businessman or your dream job with great pay, not just "I want to make more money" or "I want to be a millionaire." These are not inspiring. You have to marry the vision, which means it's a partnership. It must be something you love to do, something to bring about in this world that nobody would have to pay you to do. You must be passionate about it – something that will pull you out of bed every morning, all fired up and ready to attack the day with another step toward your vision, full of energy and motivation.

You can find your passion and do things you enjoy daily but still be broke; I know I was. I had a sign shop business in Hempstead, New York, and the Town of Hempstead was one of my customers. I made hundreds of signs for them—metal signs, banners, you name it and made lots of money from them alone. I love anything that I have to use my hands. I love making the signs, but I did not have a vision for the business. I had big accounts – schools, big businesses – earned money, but I was getting nowhere. I ended up losing most of my customers and went broke. A proverb says, "Without a vision, the people perish." We can extend that parable and say, "Without a vision, a marriage perishes, a family perishes, a career perishes, and a business will perish, too." Passion alone won't get you anywhere. You have to lock in the vision to make it happen. It will push you to get help or to take a class if you have to.

A vision is more significant than a single task or goal; it should describe the kind of person you want to be and what responsibilities and accomplishments will be necessary to make that happen. With a vision for your life, daily goals connect in a meaningful way, allowing each achievement to lay the groundwork for even bigger successes down the road. So set yourself up for success by running your day by the clock and your life with a vision, as Legendary Motivational speaker Zig Ziglar puts it.

Chapter 2

Goals

I can honestly say that I was a wandering generality in my early years living in the USA. Looking in my rearview mirror, I did not accomplish much of anything – in and out of debt, bad investments, tons of mistakes, poor credit, bad timing, no plans, no goals, no direction at all, getting up, going to work, doing the same thing day in and day out, expecting different results. I had a few side businesses taking up most of my time. I was working on everything simultaneously, chasing money and opportunities – I even left my job to pursue a dream with no plans. I failed miserably.

The reason I did not achieve what I wanted at that time wasn't that I was incapable or lacked opportunities or that some circumstances had arisen in my life. It was because I did not know what I wanted, and it's hard or almost impossible to find something when you don't know what it is. I randomly asked people what they wanted in life for the sake of writing this book. Almost all of them were confused, some told me their wishes and dreams, and others didn't know what they wanted, sleepwalking through life aiming at nothing.

The Harvard Business School reports that 3% of people in the world set goals. Only 3% know where they're heading, and the rest work for them. If you want growth in any area of your life, you must have some goals. Goals are a must, and there is no way around it. Not only will it help you achieve whatever you want in life, but having goals will give you a life, a reason to get up every morning, something to look forward to, rather than getting up in the morning going to work every day to some job that you hate, knowing that you would rather be doing something different.

You might have career, personal, or financial goals – you name it. You can have goals in different areas of your life, and you should. Staying balanced with your life is excellent, but sometimes some areas might become more critical than others. I remember listening to Kobe Bryant. At the beginning of his career, he spent most of his time focusing on a single goal - to be the best basketball player ever. He told his wife that he must work hard to achieve that goal. He had to sacrifice some personal relationship goals with his family and friends. I understand that too much of anything, even the good stuff, is not good, but sometimes you must sacrifice something to get something. But one thing I liked about Kobe was that he ensured his family knew what he was doing.

You must be detail-oriented when setting your goals. To have lots of money, a big house, a beautiful wife, or more education is way too broad to be actual goals because they're not specific enough. If maybe one of your goals is to find the right partner, then sit down and describe the right partner. Write precisely who you want your partner to be, and be as specific as possible. Write down what he or she will be like – tall or short, for instance, or maybe you have gender preference or race? Write it all down – handsome, down-to-earth, loving, caring, muscular, intelligent, and so on. Perhaps your goal is to buy a home. Take the assortment of ideas for your home and commit them to paper. How many square feet, location, number of rooms, bathrooms, style, color, wood or brick? Get a local artist to draw it for you with as much detail as possible. Get your goals out of your head and onto paper.

When I decided to write this book, I made sure I was specific enough about my goal. I wanted to write a non-fiction book, about 250 pages, 21 chapters, the topics of each chapter, the name of the book, why I'm writing the book, what's the message I'm conveying in the book, what's the whole idea behind it, how many words per chapter. I had an artist design the cover of the book. I sent it to a print shop to print it on vinyl. Then I took a book from my shelf, applied my cover, and placed it on my desk. I wanted to see the end result because it's imperative to experience what it would be like when you reach your goal – the feeling, the satisfaction, the joy. When working on your goals, you must have those feelings – the feeling that you have already achieved them.

I once got laid off while working on this book project. I spent three hours a day at the library writing this book. I had to stop that career goal as a writer for the time being because it became much less important than finding a source of income. You can't be creative on an empty stomach. I spent as much time as needed looking for a job. I did find one quick enough to resume my work on writing this book. Some goals can wait. You must prioritize when setting your goals and decide the order of importance to you because each one requires time and adjustment as you progress. Sometimes you might have to compromise or settle. At any rate, to accomplish them, you must be very organized.

Once you've arranged your goals in order of importance, you should list the obstacles that stand between you and your objectives. If there weren't any obstacles between you and your goals, you would have everything you wanted. So, after you list the obstacles, you can formulate a plan to overcome them and set a schedule. Studies show that once you correctly identify a problem, you have it half-solved. You will be amazed at how quickly you overcome the obstacles once you identify them. As you overcome the obstacles on your way to one goal, the barriers to other goals will fall more easily.

As you set your goals, let me urge you not to try to overcome all the obstacles before you start. Nobody would attempt anything of significance if all the obstacles had to be removed before they started. If you had called the Chief of Police before leaving for work this morning to inquire if all the traffic lights were green, he would have thought you were crazy. You know perfectly well that you will deal with the lights one at a time until you arrive at your destination. As you deal with the obstacles the same way, you will one day arrive at your destination. You go as fast as you can see and can always see farther when you get there. Cross the bridge when you get to the bridge, and deal with the obstacles when you get to the obstacles, not before.

Now take it on a more gradual basis. I mean, you are not going to take out the heavyweight champion, Mike Tyson, in the first year as you enter the professional ranks as a boxer. Beating the champion can be a long-range goal for any fighter who wishes to be the champion at some point in their career. So many people had destroyed their careers by getting over their heads against the competition that was too tough before they gained the necessary experience. In sales, people shoot themselves in the leg right at the start. They initially set huge goals to make a million dollars a year. The human brain isn't going to stay motivated if you can't see that you're making progress toward your goal. I am not saying that you can't set big goals. Reaching your goal should stretch you, but big goals have unique drawbacks that need extra attention and planning. Sometimes it's better to convert your lofty goals into a long-term vision while setting a smaller goal that gets you closer to it and is achievable within a reasonable time frame.

I urge you to select achievable targets within your industry or organization and find out who's right above you.

It's good to be very ambitious, and you must have big goals in life. However, the timing is crucial here. While I was training for a marathon, the New York City Marathon was coming up, and friends of mine encouraged me to sign up for it. They told me, "You can do it!" I wanted to believe that, but I couldn't. I knew I was not ready and needed more training. At that time, I was gradually progressing in my training, but I could only run ten miles before my knees and ankles started to break down. I was not strong enough to carry on to the 26th mile.

"How one can eat an Elephant - One bite at a time" Set one long-range goal and break it down into many short-range and daily goals. Writing this non-fiction book was a long-range goal for me, so I broke it down into short-range, daily goals that I would work on every day. There are 365 days in a year. I set the goal for the year to write one page a day. I think anyone can do that. It made writing the book so effortlessly, so easy for me to do that I did before the year's end. I could not procrastinate on writing because the task was easy.

Things become so easy when you organize, identify the obstacles, and formulate a plan for achieving the goal. I wrote down my obstacles at the very beginning. Not being fluent in English was my biggest problem. Since English is not my first language, I took English literature classes and read many books. I joined a couple of writing groups online to help me brainstorm topics and ideas I should write about and how to write them. Then the writing part. I was not a writer at all. I thought it was boring. So, to make it achievable, I scheduled 60 minutes a day to learn how to write and started to write by brainstorming topics. Then I started doing some research and writing about those topics. I told a guy in my writing group that sometimes I don't feel inspired to write. He advised me to write anyway. Once I get into the motion of writing, inspiration follows. I learned a great lesson that day: You don't wait until you feel like it; you have to start the process to feel like it. I wrote over 900 pages on different topics before committing to this book. I began to get excited as I was writing. Gradually I got it done.

Some goals can be damaging if they are out of your field of interest or if you are trying to please someone. It's doubtful that reaching that goal will be completely free of resentment. The goal has to be exciting, engaging, inspiring, and motivating. You have to want it. You can't wait to achieve it. The goal has to be something that will change you. Setting a goal to make a million-dollar sale in your business is fine, but getting the million dollars is not important here. What's important is who you had to become to make that million. Even if you lose the money after you make it, you can always get it back because now you know what to do and how to do it. So, who you become in the process of achieving that goal is the key reason why you should set a goal that will push your limits and get you out of your comfort zone – that's where change happens.

Jacob Braude once wrote, "life is like a grindstone. It can polish you up or grind you down. It all depends on how you position yourself." We all have desires, passions, dreams, and aspirations, but very few set or write down goals. When we see the very few people on earth that do, we tend to have the utmost admiration for them because they live at the desired destination of the next level. You can win by just setting your goals daily. And when those goals are executed and the dreams become a reality, a frown quickly turns into a smiley face. Without goals and plans, your life stands still like a statue.

How can you hit a target that you don't even have? Whether your goals are short or long, you must give yourself direction by creating and implementing a plan. And once that plan is in place, you instantly have a clear vision that you can stand tall with your head up high. Now you know what to do and when to do it. The choice is always yours. A dream without a goal is just a dream, so if you refuse to set goals, you might as well go to sleep. But make it a deep sleep so the dream will seem more real.

Most people don't ever achieve what they want in life. It's not because they are incapable or lack opportunities or circumstances and events have arisen in their lives. Most people never define what they want in life, and finding something is impossible when you don't know what you are looking for. You are not reaching your full potential if you haven't got a target. If you haven't got a goal, you will never achieve your dream because the chance of you one day falling into your dream is right around nothing. Some people might say their goal is to be successful – "I just want to be successful!" or "I just want to be rich!" These are not goals – these are wishes, and wishes do not come true. You must be specific, know exactly what you want, learn how you will get it, and work until you get it. Define what you want, write it down and read it to yourself daily. Let it sink into your subconscious mind. You must go out there and seize your dream. You got to say, "This is what I want, and this is how I'm going to get it, and I will do whatever it takes!"

Huge goals can be damaging, but too small goals can also demotivate. If your goals are easy to achieve, they are not big enough. Set bigger goals, goals that excite you and scare you at the same time. If it is important to you, you will make it happen; if it's not, you will find an excuse. How bad do you want it? Some say they set goals but don't take action toward them because they get overwhelmed. Take that "impossible" goal and break it down into small steps you can take to build some momentum. Once you get going, you won't be able to stop, and you will achieve your goal. Then you can move on to the next level – bigger targets, greater accomplishments.

Find a profound emotional reason, your WHY, your reason that ensures you will never back down when times get hard. The world is full of opportunities for anyone – race or gender. In this 21st century, with the advancement of technology, you can be anywhere in this world and still make a fortune. Each of us is sitting on a pot of gold, ideas that can change our life, but very few decide to act on them, write them down, set goals and achieve them.

The South African-born Elon Musk aims to send one million people to Mars by 2050 by launching three starship rockets daily and creating many jobs on the Red Planet. He shares his goals on Twitter. Most people say he's nuts and unrealistic; his goals are absurd and don't make sense. Why would anyone want to go to Mars? After selling PayPal to eBay for $1.5 billion, he went to Russia to prospect for rockets because he heard Russians had them for sale. The Russians were asking for too much for them, so he decided to build his own with a friend. He said he went to the library and read almost every book about rockets. Knowledge, when applied, is power. That's precisely what Elon did. Anything is possible.

Never fight your limitation when setting goals. I can't do this; I'm not smart enough; this is out of my league; I'm broke; I need more information before I get started. When you acknowledge your limitations, you get to keep them.

Goals have the power to change you. Most people won't end up where they want to be because they never define where that place is. They drift through life with no direction, and then they wonder why they are in the middle of no-where. Don't be like that; you know better than that. Be like the very few who know where they are going in life, the very few who desire to work on and improve every area, are excited at the possibility, and are looking forward to each level.

Chapter 3

Plan ahead

Three fish lived in a pond. One was named Plan Ahead, another was Think Fast, and the third was Wait and See. One day they heard a fisherman say that he would cast his nets into their pond the next day. Plan Ahead said, "I'm swimming down the river tonight!" Think Fast said, "I'm sure I'll come up with a plan." Wait and See lazily said, "I just can't think about it now!" When the fisherman cast his nets, Plan Ahead was long gone. But Think Fast and Wait and See were caught! Think Fast quickly rolled his belly up and pretended to be dead. "Oh, this fish is no good!" said the fisherman, throwing him safely back into the water. But Wait and See ended up in the fish market. That is why they say, "In times of danger when the net is cast, plan ahead or plan to think fast!".Before you go to bed tonight, have a game plan for tomorrow written out every step of the way. Be on schedule, and don't be late when it comes to you. One day, I told my coach that I am never on time when it comes to me, meaning if I schedule my time to do a task at 3:00 pm, I am usually late. I got the job done, but not when I was expected to do it.

"That's not good enough; hold yourself accountable when it comes to you. You don't like to be late for work at your day job, why are you making your employer more important than you? Schedule it and be on time. Don't ever be late again," said my coach Bob

In the book, Breaking the Habit of Being Yourself, the author, Dr. Joe Dispenza, said, "Lose your mind and create a new one." That changed Everything for me going forward. I read that 450-page book in two days. I was so in tune with what he was saying that it sounded like he was talking to me. At some point in the book, it almost seemed like he was saying, "Papa, if you want to change your life and get better results, you will have to become a new person. I wanted better results, so I took him up on that. That led me to hire coach Bob to help me reach my goals.

I could not afford Coach Bob when we first started. I went into debt because of that; I had to put up three credit cards to pay for it, but to stay on the path I was following then, I could not afford not to hire him. And my life changed from that point on. I began to see clearly where I was heading and what I was doing wrong.

I want to learn from someone else's mistakes, someone who has already traveled the same path I'm trying to take. I want to follow and pay him to teach me – hold my hand, save me time and money, and get better results faster.

All successful people have coaches. A friend of mine has four coaches. He told me that when he is on a new journey, a new goal that he's trying to reach, to save himself some time, he goes and hires a coach or a mentor – someone who's more experienced in that field to guide him.

Plan tomorrow before tomorrow gets here; know where tomorrow's time will be allocated. Avoid getting up in the morning with no plan for the day; that will be a day wasted, as Jim Rohn puts it.

Work from a calendar standpoint, stated Coach Bob. I should know what I intend to do every day for the next 90 days. Tasks should be specific and detail-oriented in accordance with my goals. I didn't have a plan for any day before I met him, never wrote anything down. I was going with the flow, figuring things out on the fly. A whole lot has changed since then. If the task is not on my calendar, I won't entertain it. Running errands or going to Home Depot, my favorite store, it's already scheduled on the calendar.

I have a friend I usually call for help. I'm considerate enough to call people ahead of time so they can pencil me in their calendars, but this particular guy, every time I call him for some help, always checks his calendar before he gives me an answer. I love him; he's very busy. That's why I ask him for help when I need help. "If you want something done, give it to a busy guy because the guy who has all the time in the world tends to keep it that way, not doing anything.".

The best way to improve is to review. Put up the day for review at the end of every day. Basketball players do it all the time. They watch the game tape after the game. You should do the same thing with your days, review the day in the end, and find out what went wrong. What went right? Did I follow my plan? Was I prepared enough? What have I learned that will help me tomorrow?

Save time, not money; more time can get you more money. Time is the ultimate commodity. You need time to be in a good relationship; you need time to grow a business. Hire a coach to help you save time. Two minds are better than one.

Picture yourself going into a jungle full of monkeys; your goal is to catch ten monkeys. How would you go about catching them? Would you try to catch them all at the same time? If so, you will never catch any of them."

I was all over the place, a wandering generality with a full-time job and five side hustles always broke. It was ridiculous. Running all these sides hustle just me alone won't get you anywhere, as my brother told me. And he was so right!!! He usually came by to lecture me, I hated it, but that was what I needed to hear. I was determined to get my life in order, to work on a schedule, and to be very specific when setting goals. I listened to lots of motivational tapes. I went to countless seminars. I met the legendary motivational speaker and business strategist Tony Robbins in Canada, which was awesome. I was hyped about leaving that seminar. I loved it. After seeing and hearing Tony Robbins, I told my good friend Henock on our way back from Canada, "I have to get my life together, get my head fixed on something and stay on course to the end."

Suppose you make your plans every evening for the following day. In that case, you will not wake up in the morning like a chicken head cut off, be all over the place, about to repeat what you did yesterday, wasting your time, doing the same mundane tasks, and expecting different results – that's the definition of insanity. Be hard on yourself, and schedule your time.

You see, what you focus on expands. If you are the complaining type, you will never run out of things to complain about. For me, life is great, and life is also deserving. I work, and I get paid. I'm always looking for ways to grow. I have to get something in return for my time invested. Time is the only thing that I have. You need time to earn money, and you need time to do anything in life, so use your time wisely. I think your time should be scheduled every day to the minute. Now I'm exaggerating maybe a little bit, but be aware of how you spend your time. You should think of your time like money in the bank. You can't just spend it willy-nilly. You should save it, protect it, and invest it where you can get more time for your money. I try to invest time to get money, and once I get the money, I can buy other people time to help me do things better and faster with less time. Buy a calendar at the office supply, and Ask yourself what the most important things you value the most are. Mine is: Family, health and wellness, business and career, and spirituality.

From 0 to 10, what's your score in these areas?

My score was:

Family 4/10

Health and wellness 8/10

Business and career 3/10

Spirituality 7/10

The family score was very low for me, 4/10, because I thought I was not spending enough time with family; I was not calling or seeing my brothers, sisters, and friends caused I was always working. I sat down to write goals in that area. What can I do in this area to score 9 or 10/10? I wrote the things I needed to do, scheduled them in my calendar, and took action. Business and career, also I scored very low, I was broke, and I was not supposed to be broke because I live in the wealthiest land in the world, the USA; like singer Alicia Keys said, if you can't make it here, you won't make it anywhere. Time to man up and get the money. I went into learning mode, coaching, and reading to improve; I scheduled the time and took action. I was living paycheck to paycheck; now I have forgotten the pay period; I am hanging out with the Jefferson now.

I use a 90-day rolling calendar, which works like this: I look at the next 90 days – May, June, and July, for instance. In those three months, I make sure anything that has to do with the family goes into the calendar – family and friends' birthdays, road trips (my wife's favorite thing to do), etc. She loves massages and stuff, so I put them on the calendar. Gym time: Everything goes on the calendar – business goals, book writing, library time, coaching time, reading time, working on becoming a speaker, reading and understanding the Coran and Bible. My goal is to book the next 90 days. And once the time is scheduled, it becomes a commitment; just like a doctor's appointment, I must get it done.

At the end of every month, I look at the next 90 days, and at the end of every week, I look at the next two weeks, and at the end of every day, I look at the next two days. I am always looking ahead, fine-tuning everything I have to do. That purpose is to ensure that my highest priorities are scheduled. That way, I see myself progressing and moving toward my goals, and I'm starting to feel better about myself. Progress equals Happiness.

Nobody ever wrote down a plan to be broke, fat, lazy, or stupid. Those things are what happen when you don't have a plan.

Chapter 4

Perception

*There is no good or bad without us
There is only perception. There is the event
itself and the story we tell ourselves about what
it means*

After a long shift, James was too tired to drive his 1998 Volkswagen home. Instead of catching a ride with a coworker or getting a taxi, he decided to drive himself. But, a few minutes later, he ended up in a ditch. He felt embarrassed and was blaming himself. But instead of feeling sorry, he decided to take action. He walked out of his car and asked a nearby farmer for help. You need a team of young stallions to pull up that car said the farmer. I have only one horse. His name is Dusty; he's blind and old. We'll bring him over to see what he can do but don't expect too much.

The farmer hitched Dusty to the car, snapped a whip

in the air, and said, "Pull, Jimmy, pull!" Dusty never moved. The farmer snapped the whip again and said, "Pull, Sammy, pull!" Dusty still did not move. The farmer snapped the whip a third time and said, "Pull, Charley, pull!" but Dusty remained still. The farmer cracked the whip a fourth time and said, "Pull, Dusty, pull!" With one mighty tug, Dusty yanked the car out of the ditch.

James shook the farmer's hand and said, "Thanks for freeing my car, but there is something I don't understand. Dusty never moved when you kept calling him by those different names. Why didn't you call Dusty by his name from the start?" The farmer replied, "I had to call out those other three names first. Dusty is blind. If he'd thought he had to do all that work alone, he never would've even tried."

Don't let your perception limit you.

I came to the USA in 1999, big problem – I could not put two English words together. I was dropped off at my brother's house in Delaware. The University of Delaware's library is on Campus, said my brother; you can head over there, watch some movies, and kill some time until I get back from class. Luckily that day, when I got to the library, they had these small color T.V.s attached to a VCR to watch tapes. It was cool, and I loved it.

The first movie I watched was New Jack City. I noticed that the spoken words were written on the screen when the movie was playing. I was amazed by that. It was the closed captions; I did not know. I capitalized on that. Because of that, I was at the library every day, watching various movies to learn English. I figured out very early that if I wanted to grow in this country, I would first learn how to speak the language. I went to work on that – reading books, watching movies, and talking to people.

To speak like a native American was unbelievable for me at first. It's going to take a very long time. I was not born in the U.S., and it's not easy to learn a new language at my age." I had a lot of doubts about my ability to learn, and my entourage was not helping me either. I was hanging with two African students from Ghana who never stopped making fun of my accent. One told me to stick to the French, and the other said, "English is not for me; I was terrible." I'm laughing now as I'm writing this book.

In 2016, my biggest goal was to write a book to share my personal experiences in the USA. At first, I thought of writing just a little booklet, like a few pages, and being done with it because I did not think I could write a 300-page book. I do read a lot. At first, the goal was perceived as out of my league. I was telling myself, who am I to write the book? I'm not good enough, I'm not smart enough, and I don't have a Ph.D. Despite people, friends, and family motivating me, I was fighting my limitations every day, telling me I was smart enough and could be an author.

I took a huge interest in public speaking through my coach. I was invited to join the Toastmasters International Club in Manhattan. Toastmasters is an organization that teaches public speaking and leadership skills through a worldwide network of clubs. Warren Buffet, the world's richest man, said everyone should learn to communicate appropriately in public.

There is a club in almost every town in the U.S. and worldwide. The Manhattan club meets every Tuesday. I still remember my first day; I was the only guest. Every club has something they call "Table Topics," mainly for guests. You get a call to the podium to introduce yourself, and the host will ask you a few random questions, and you're expected to answer right there. That's what they call "learning to think on your feet." So when they called my name to come to the podium, I started to sweat. I'm not kidding; I was so nervous; I did not know they would put me on the spot like that.

It was the first time I ever stood up in front of an audience, speaking. It was brutal weeks after that, but I managed to give ten speeches over the next few months. I earned my Competence Communicator Certificate. Can you believe that? I went from not knowing English to teaching myself watching movies with closed captioning. There is no way I could believe I could be the best speaker in my group, compete for the world's best speaker, and write a book.

I stumbled into my strength. My eyes started to get bigger. If I could do this, what else could I do?

Don't let your current perception limit you.

Albert Einstein said, "The most important decision we make as humans is whether we believe we live in a friendly or hostile universe." Your eyes see, your brain translates, and your mind perceives. You see things all day, but your perception gives your life meaning. So, when you perceive, you generate a meaningful interpretation that fits your worldview. This is the most potent truth regarding the story you have about yourself. You create a story with your perception of the world, and that story becomes you. That same story can be given to you by your family, culture, school system, or entourage. Your story may create feelings of pleasure, sensations, or pain, but it all comes from your perception. Since you're the only person with control over what's in that story, you alone have the power to change it. The question is, how? Perception is everything. We choose how we look at things. We retain the ability to inject perspective into a situation. We can't change the obstacles, but we have the power of perception to decide how the obstacle will appear.

Growing up in Senegal, West Africa, where the world perceives you as poor, frail, ignorant, and hungry. Some people even told me that it must be like heaven for me to live in America. I used to laugh at that. Since you form the story or the perception you hold about your life, choosing to become the artist of your own life opens you up to unimagined experiences.

There is a corny metaphor, but it's true. There was this guy at the circus who had this giant elephant. He put this little rope around the elephant's neck and drove a stake into the ground. If you looked, you'd know that the elephant could rip down the entire circus tent almost without effort, yet the elephant did not struggle or try. Why? Because the elephant is conditioned. He had conditioned the elephant ever since he was a calf. It did not have much power when it was a baby elephant. So, they put a big rope around his neck, and they drove this huge stake into the ground, and the elephant fought and fought to get loose but could not. Finally, one day, the elephant decided, "I'm not capable of pulling this out." In this case, he won't even try anymore.

You might think, "It's just who I am, that's how it is, that's just the way it is in my life." Please look at any place where you've perceived a limitation and ask yourself when you decided to accept that limitation and raise your standards. When you start overthinking or over-calculating, you believe the most limited thoughts. Your brain is not designed to make you happy; it's designed to make you survive. Your mind will do whatever it takes to stop you from doing the unknown or taking risks. It wants to keep you in your comfort zone, where it controls things. That's why it's always hard to try new things or habits. Your mind doesn't know what to do at first, so it fights you to revert to familiarity, what it already knows.

The perceiving eyes see the obstacles. It brings our issues to the fight. Being superficial, as Nietzsche said, taking things only at first glance is the most profound approach. How often did you apply judgment to things we don't control, as though there was a way they were supposed to be?

Observing eyes see what's there, clear of distraction, exaggerations, and misperception. It removes us, the subjective part, from the equation.

It's so much better when we see things as they are, not as we've made them in our minds. We always know what others should do to fix their issues. Their problems are crystal clear to us. The solution is obvious. But when it comes to us. It's messy, crippling, scary, and hard to solve. Perception is the problem; it gives us the information we don't exactly need at the moment when it would be far better to focus on what is immediately in front of us.

Our perspective is the framework of our forthcoming response. Where the head goes, the body follows. Right action always follows the right perspective.

Chapter 5

Habits

The cardinal Rule of Behavior Change
"What's get rewarded gets repeated.
What's get punished, gets avoided"

W hen I got married, I told my wife, "Listen, don't do laundry on Wednesdays or Saturdays, alright?" She was so puzzled she asked, "Why not?" My response was, "I was told not to" Ask my mom. In Africa, parents are like God. Children take orders from them, never challenge them. So my wife asked. It turned out that my mom got it from her mom, who told her that if you do laundry on Wednesdays or Saturdays, you would always struggle through life. That's absurd, of course, ridiculously stupid. I couldn't believe she got me to do that based on that old nonsense grandmother's tale. Someone said that the apple does not fall too far from the tree. You tend to mirror the habits of people close to you – your parents, friends, entourage, and circle of influence.

Growing up, it wasn't easy to find a role model. We modeled the habits of the culture, and we did not know whether it was good or bad for us.

Too often, you follow the habits of your culture without thinking about or questioning them.

As the French philosopher Michel de Montaigne wrote, "The customs and practice of life in society sweep us along. Most of the time, going along with the group does not feel like a burden. Everyone wants to belong somewhere."

Liposuction is a technique in cosmetic surgery for removing excess fat from under the skin by suction. It has become trendy lately. That's the way to go if you want to shred fat quickly. I know people that did it, and their bodies changed drastically. I was impressed by it. Guess what? Every single gram of fat removed came right back within a few months. Like lottery winners, they become a millionaire overnight; check them in a couple of years, and all the money is gone. Being broke or fat is never a problem. We think we need to change our results, but the results aren't the problem. It's the system that caused the results that we should address. Fix the inputs, and the outputs fix themselves. The score always takes care of itself. You don't rise to the level of your goal. You fall to the level of your systems, and that's where you should put all your focus, as James Clear puts it in his book Atomic Habits.

Habits are the difference, nothing else. Routines, things that you constantly do, will make the difference. Your outcomes in life are often the measure of your habits. The bank accounts, the test scores, or the numbers on the scale must change; the things that need to be changed are the habits that precede those outcomes. Rather than making the goals the default, the things you focus on exclusively, let's make the system the default and only check occasionally to see if we're moving in the right direction. Achieving your goals only changes your life for the moment; it's not the things you are looking for.

For example, if you have a messy bedroom, you set a goal to clean that room. You can get motivated to clean it up, and in an hour, you will have a clean room – for now. But if you don't change the messy habits that led to a messy room in the first place, you will turn around two weeks later, and you will have a messy room again. You don't need to keep cleaning your room – you need a better cleaning habit, and your room will always be clean. You don't need to lose weight; you need better eating habits, and the weight will always be where you want it to be. You don't need more money – you need better financial habits, and then you will have enough money to manage the things that come up.

Put a new system in place and run it. Losing weight or making money should never be the goal. Being healthy or having financial freedom should be the goal, where you will force yourself to build the habits of a healthy person or the habits of a wealthy person.

Small habits matter so much because they change who you are. Yes, they don't necessarily transform your life overnight but gradually transform your identity. For example, doing one push-up won't transform your body, but it will cast a vote for being the person who does not miss a workout. Meditating for five minutes might not give you an immediate sense of calm, but it does cast a vote for being a meditator. The real goal is not being in a marathon. It's becoming a runner. The goal is not to write a book but to become a writer. Because once you adopt that identity, you're not pursuing a behavior change; you act in alignment with the kind of person you've already seen yourself as. An actual behavior change is like an identity change. Once you transform that internal story, it's easier to show up each day without motivating yourself to do it. You will feel like, This Is Who I Am.

True long-term thinking is goalless thinking. When you focus on being that person, developing that identity, and following that system, you realize your potential along the way. Every action you take is like a vote for the person you want to become, and if you can master the right action and right habits, then you can start to cast a vote for this new identity, this desired person that you want to be.

Good habits can become easy when you learn to find joy in delayed gratification. When you develop that mindset, there is no rush built for the long term.

It is challenging to build better habits because they are effortless to dismiss on any given day. What is the difference between eating a burger and fries for lunch or a salad? Not a whole lot on any given day; your body looks the same in the mirror, and the scale has stayed the same. It's easy to dismiss in your mind and say, "Oh, this is insignificant," but you turn around two, five, or ten years later and realize, "Oh, wow, those daily choices do add up!" It's just much harder to see a transformation on a granular basis. The cost of your good habits is in the present, and the cost of your bad habits is in the future, and the fact that we prioritize the present over the future makes habit change difficult.

Many people think that they lack motivation – what they lack is clarity. They believe that they need to get motivated and that they need the willpower to execute good habits. If I waited until I felt like writing, working out, or meditating, I would be waiting for a long time to do those things. The problem is most people don't have a plan. They wake up each day thinking, "I wonder if I feel motivated to write today? Or if I will feel motivated to work out today?" Instead, you can take the decision-making out by explicitly stating when, where, and how you want to implement the habits and then do them.

In his book You are the placebo, Joe Dispenza said that to break a habit, you have to be a different person. He meant that you need to divorce your current habits and adhere to new ones by implementing new habits, putting a new system in place, and running it. Habits are the difference between rich and poor – the poor person has poor habits that keep him poor; it's that simple.

It's hard to eliminate the bad habits that keep you average, always in debt and complaining. That's because you have been on autopilot all of your life, doing the same things daily without much thought. Your days are the same for months and years. It will be challenging for you to change because it will require you to be present to involve your mind to help you navigate through it, and it will require willpower, determination, and a tremendous amount of discipline to change direction.

People develop countless habits as they navigate the world, whether they are aware of them or not. The knee-jerk nature of these behaviors can help people meet their needs more efficiently in everyday life. Yet the fact that habits become deeply ingrained in our brains means that even if a particular habit creates more problems than it solves, it can be challenging to break. Understanding how habits take shape, to begin with, may help dismantle and replace them.

I am reminded of a famous story about a prank that college students played on their professor. As the story goes, the professor was known for "talking with his hands" and making lots of gestures while explaining concepts to students.

On the first day of the semester, a few students met amongst themselves and agreed that whenever the professor raised his arms while talking, the students would nod their heads and smile approvingly at whatever he said. The students followed through on their plan, and by the end of the term, the professor was gesticulating with such vigor that his arms were flailing wildly throughout the entire lecture.

We learn which behaviors to repeat based on how they make us feel. When we take an action that feels good—like a professor looking at a room full of students smiling and nodding—we want to do more of that action in the future: The cardinal rule of behavior change is: What is rewarded gets repeated.

It takes work to do things that are beneficial to me. It's so ironic and stupid when your mind is working against you to a degree. Your mind wants it easy, so it always tells you to keep doing what you've been doing. It doesn't like change because change requires thinking, doing new things, and changing new routes. It's always easy to take the same route home because you don't need to think, and your mind is already programmed on that route. That's why you need to break the habit of being yourself. I put my watch on my right wrist, while most people put it on their left wrist.

I do that to break a pattern in my mind, to keep my mind working differently. I take different routes to go to work or to come home. I'm always doing something new to break the cycle because once it's broken, your mind is forced to build a new cycle that requires thinking and will force the change.

Once I reach my goal, I will be happy, so I put off happiness until then. I did that for years. I was stressed out.   I was showing little progress for months. I was on a goal-oriented mindset instead of a system-first mentality. The sole purpose of setting a goal is to win the game. The purpose of building systems is to continue playing the game. It's about the cycle of endless refinement and continuous improvement.Fall in love with the process, not the end goal.

What is punished is avoided. Put a system in motion every day and run it. You can be satisfied anytime your system is running "The best thing about the future is that it comes one day at a time," as US President Abraham Lincoln puts it.

A better life requires a better system. Old habits can be difficult to shake up, and good habits are often harder to develop. But through repetition, it's possible to form and maintain new habits. Even habits that have been harmful to one's health and well-being for a long time can be changed with enough determination and a smart approach.

Chapter 6

Unlock the prison
of your Mind

A citizen was arrested by one of the barons. He was taken down dark stairs, down, down, down, by a ferocious-looking jailer who carried a great key a foot long. When they reached the cell, its door was opened, and the jailer thrust the man into a dark hole. Then he shut the door with a bang, leaving the prisoner in that dark dungeon in the baron's castle. For the next twenty years, the jailer would come once a day, opening the big door with a great creaking and groaning and thrusting a pitcher of water and a loaf of bread.

For twenty years, the prisoner endured his life in those terrible conditions. And after that long time, he decided he could not stand it any longer. He wanted to die, but he did not want to commit suicide. So, he decided that the next day when the jailer came, he would attack him. The jailer would then kill him in self-defense, and thus his misery would end. He thought he would examine the door carefully to be ready for tomorrow, and, going over, he caught the handle and turned it. To his amazement, the door opened, and he found no lock on it and never had been. For all those twenty years, he had not been locked in at all except in his own belief. At any time in that period, he could have opened the door if only he had known it wasn't locked. He groped along the corridor and felt his way upstairs. At the top of the stairs, he saw two soldiers. However, they were chatting and made no attempt to stop him. He crossed the great yard without attracting attention. There was an armed guard on the drawbridge at the great gate, but they paid no attention to him, and he walked out a free man. He went home unmolested and lived happily ever after. He could have done this at any time through those long years since his arrest if he had known enough, but he did not. He was captive, not of stone and iron, but of false belief. He was not locked in; he only thought he was. Of course, this is a legend, but it is highly instructive.

It seems strange that one who has never been in a "real" prison should be pontificating to those incarcerated! However, those "inside" and "outside" have more in common than one might imagine. And what works to bring peace to one applies to all, no matter the seeming difference in outer circumstances. The mind, at times, can be worse than a physical prison; worry and fear can take us into a dark state of panic, and the world can feel like a terrifying place.

We all live in some prison - some in prison of misfortune, unintelligence, fear, or sickness. But always, the prison has no power in time or conditions to make us old, tired or sick.

The things we embrace, observe and see between the ages of zero and eight affect our worldview. It determines what's available to us and what's not available to us. Studies said our unconscious mind governs 90% of our behavior that we've embraced and learned from our parents, teachers, environment, or people that we saw. Thus, your environmental game is more important than your mental game. If you want to see a drastic change, change your environment and the people you associate with or listen to, and everything will change. Your entourage is everything because your network is your net worth. You will likely be like the people you spend most of your time with. You will surely be the tenth if you hang out with nine broke people. The opposite is true: if you hang out with nine rich people, you will be the tenth. That's a law just like the law of gravity – it always works. I read many books on personal development and learned about influencing, changing my state, and thinking differently.

I have been to a lot of educational events. Why do so many people go to all these self-improvement and personal development events and get all excited just to lose their motivation when they come back home? They cannot maintain their excitement because the environment overrides all the changes they experienced, and life slowly starts to drift back to normal. The environment has to support what you're doing, which you need to address. The most powerful force I'm aware of in this world is the need to be consistent and congruent with the expectations of our peer group. Iron sharpens iron.

Your mind gravitates towards which it's most familiar. So if you're familiar with worrying and focusing on problems, these are your dominating thoughts. Your mind gravitates toward this type of thought, and you produce just that, a life full of chaos, doubts, and failure. You become what you are thinking about, and most people think about what they don't want. I don't want this; I hate that; I hate my life, my job, and so on. Take out "I don't want" in your vocabulary, and forget about what you don't want. Just talk about what you want.

The mind will come up with plenty of exaggerated and unrealistic ideas that are unlikely ever to materialize. Still, when locked in a prison of thought, these ideas seem real and tend to cause great suffering. Negative thoughts can create anxiety and mental pain because we live with our thoughts in our minds as though they are happening in reality.

So, by making a statement such as "It's hard, it's tough, I will never make it here," you're creating your own prison. The mind works miraculously. If you are trying to do something and all the time you are saying, "It's hard, there is no way out of this, it's impossible," – guess what? Your mind won't even try because the mind works on statements. If the statement you made is "it's hard," then why even try? Never fight your limitations because you get to keep them.

We see the world differently because of one word, "Paradigm." A paradigm is a framework of thought, a scheme for understanding and explaining certain aspects of reality. Paradigm explains the world to us. It's the basic way of thinking, perceiving, valuing, and doing associated with a particular vision of reality. If you believe in a paradigm, a pattern, or a fact about yourself, that paradigm will start running your life. I read the book Paradign by Joel Arthur Baker, great book; he said:

A paradigm is a set of rules and regulations, written or unwritten, that does two things:

1. It establishes or defines boundaries

2. It tells you how to behave inside the boundaries to be successful.

If you were born in a third-world country, grew up in poverty, your family does not have any money and hear the language of poverty every day. People complain that life is hard, it's tough, it's not fair, and money is hard to get; growing up with these limited beliefs is creating rules and regulations called paradigms for you to operate; it's forming your world. That paradigm will run you to the ground. You will grow up thinking that life is hard, and it's not. You inherit the paradigm of your family or your culture, and you will behave accordingly, growing up thinking and acting small, and that will keep reinforcing your limited beliefs that life is hard.

It's like some computer software that tells you how you

should think, act, and behave. Most likely, it will tell you how to kill your dreams – don't bother thinking big, it's not going to work anyway, don't expect big things because you don't deserve it, you are not good enough, not smart enough – and that kind of thinking will keep generations in poverty.

It does not matter how big, intelligent, or educated you are; if you think small, you will always get small stuff. Most people's ambitions are very small, so they remain small. I wanted to work for NASA and be an astronaut. It was a dream to go to another planet. My entourage killed that dream very quickly. Whatever you and I have done up to this point is a duplication, a reproduction of what we believe subconsciously that we deserve and what's possible for our life.

Before April 1954, the common belief was that man was not physically capable of running a mile in less than four minutes. Breaking this four-minute barrier seemed impossible because many people had tried it repeatedly and failed. So, it had never been done on the planet. However, in 1954 Roger Bannister came along and broke the four-minute barrier. What happened next? From that day up to this day, over 20,000 people have done it, including high school kids. 20,000 people! The difference was that when they got on the track, they knew running a mile in less than four minutes had been done before. So, they had a new belief that they could accomplish this goal. If someone has done it, so can you.

So, get out of your own prison. You have to change your mind about your problems and keep it changed. By changing your mind about your issues, you are building a new mental equivalent of harmony and success.

There is a story of a man who died and was shown around heaven by St Peter. They came to what St. Peter called the "heavenly Junkyard."

"Here, you will find all the gifts from heaven," he explained, "that people on earth rejected."

"Why is this impossible!?" exclaimed the newcomer, "Some of these things are beautiful. Look at the Cadillac over there. Who could possibly reject that?"

"Well, interestingly, you should ask about that particular car," replied St Peter. "As it happens, the person who rejected that Cadillac is you."

"Impossible!" protested the other, "I'd never have refused such a wonderful gift."

"All the same, it was you. The Cadillac was ready and waiting to be delivered to you. You kept praying for a Cadillac but did not believe you could get one. The mind is the first place you receive anything in life.

You can only have what you've already had. Stop praying for what you don't have. "God, Please help me pay my rent this month!! God, please, I'm begging you!" I used to pray just like that out of a consciousness of lack; that's why I was in lack for a while. I had a poverty mindset, and the law said you could only have more of what you are. I was attracting more poverty. That's why the poor get poorer.

Rev Ike said, "You can't have what you don't have." If you don't have it in your mind, you won't have it in your life. Whatever you say you are, you will remain just that. It's so important to stand guard over the door of your mind. Watch what you say to yourself when you're by yourself. That inner conversation is crucial to your success. If you keep telling yourself that you're not deserving, you're poor; you're not smart enough or listening to other losers, you will reap just that. You can not operate from a consciousness of lack expecting to be successful. Cultivate, imagine a prosperous life for you and live it in your mind. The feeling is vital here. Acting and feeling like a prosperous citizen are impressed onto the subconscious mind, and the subconscious mind will never fail to express what's been impressed upon it.

What would the feeling be like if it were true? You're now the man you would like to be, catch that success feeling and live it. Most people put it just the opposite. They say I will feel so good if I have a million dollars. However, the feeling precedes fortune.

Be joyful now with what you have. You can't say, "When I have enough money, then I will be joyful." The feeling of joy precedes the money. You get joyful and grateful first with your present condition; then, a more joyous feeling will come knocking at your door.

A mental equivalent is consistently demonstrated. The secret of success and harmony is concentrating your thoughts on harmony and success. Every time you encounter a mean, nasty person, they are unhappy. Something happened to them inside. You can't be happy inside and mean outside. That's why you must feel that joy and happiness first before people can see it in you. If you are happy, you act happy; if you are mad, you act mad; it's that simple.

So the key to life is to build the mental equivalent of what you want and expunge the equivalents of what you don't want.

OK, so how do you do that? Start by thinking quietly, constantly, and persistently about the kind of things that you want. That thinking has two qualities: Clearness and Interest. If you're going to bring health, the right job, inspiration, right companionship to your life – you have to form a mental equivalent of the thing you want by thinking about it a great deal, by thinking clearly and with interest. Remember, clarity and interest are the two poles.

The feeling is essential here. You have to feel as if you are already successful. Your desires are not subconsciously accepted until you assume the feeling of their reality. The outside mirrors the inside. You have to claim it inside before seeing it on the outside. Claiming means that you act like the successful person you want to become and start training your mind to succeed; it's all in mind; feel it.

Save the money and buy a first-class ticket to go somewhere new. This is how you train your mind to be successful. Try things you've never done before. Get an upgrade whenever you can start asking for the best and nothing but the best. When you go out, make sure you eat at the best places and save money to treat yourself to a nice dinner at an upscale restaurant. I flew business class going to China and Japan. It was a 15-hour, non-stop flight to Japan from NYC. You are in and out of the plane before the masses, wider seating, free internet, and better food. You get an email asking what you want to eat on the plane three days before your flight. I watched movies and then slept like a baby. The level of comfort was excellent.

When you treat yourself as a first-class citizen, you are conditioning your mind to behave and do things to produce first-class results. That's what Dick Gregory said. Whenever you can treat yourself to first class, do it because you will be painting a new picture, a new standard for the mind to follow. You are telling your mind, this is how I want you to behave. Next time you shop for new clothes, set the standard, and pick the best clothes.

It's all in mind, and we all have that same tool. Some people use it to condition themselves to attract success, but others lock themselves in mediocrity, in the prison of their minds, and throw the key in the ocean.

Business success coach Don Peña said it best. He was so broke when he had just started to build his empire. But he used to go to the Lamborghini dealership to test drive the new Lamborghini. He invested in nice suits to make himself feel and look successful. You'll notice that when you dress up very nicely, you tend to think better or more successful thoughts. People also react differently to you.

I saw this 26-year-old woman on YouTube talking to Tony Robbins, the business strategist. She said she was part of an epidemic of graduate students out of college with huge student loans, knowing they won't be able to make payments for the next 20 years. Tony told her that sometimes we just need to listen to ourselves. He said that there once was a man who said that if you tell a lie big enough, loud enough, and long enough, soon enough, people will believe it. His name was Adolf Hitler. We are Hitler to ourselves. If you tell yourself that you are part of an epidemic, that you are not good enough or intelligent enough, it's the same as telling yourself that you are not in control, that it's not me, it's the epidemic, and the more you tell that story, the more you believe it. The answer to your problem could be right in front of you, but you won't even see it.

Interrupt the negative story you sell to yourself every day. Working to create a new story for yourself, you begin writing a new chapter in your life.

Check this out; you're perfect at this level you are now, but if you want to grow, your current self is not qualified to take you to the next level. The next level of results requires the next level of thinking. Feed your mind, invest in it. Stop believing that negative situations come from outside of yourself. It's not people, circumstances, or events that have caused the negative situations in your life. "Nothing is inherently good or bad, but thinking makes it so," as Shakespeare told us.

The thinking was made to order what you want in life, not to indulge in it. The mind is there to receive the order and make it appear to you. However, a single thought, positive or negative, becomes a powerhouse when you believe it. Most people believe their thoughts as though they were facts, which explains why life is stressful and challenging for many.

If you believe your limiting thoughts, they will become your reality.

We give our attention to what we don't want, expecting it to change our problems. , However, when you focus on the problems and resist them, you energize them. So, they expand, becoming bigger and bigger, and distract you from solving them. The opposite tactic works better. I heard somebody once say that problems are like an unwelcome guest: if you don't give the guests any attention, they will leave!

Next, you must focus on the present, not the past or future. The mind is rarely in the present. It's always wondering what might happen, what could happen, doubting yourself, and trying to keep you in your comfort zone to keep you safe. Focus on what you have, not what you don't have.

Decide on what you want, and figure out what you do have right now to move forward. Don't wait until you receive what you think you're missing before you act. Act now with what you have.

Next, you must do things differently and borrow a new mindset. If you keep doing what you've been doing, you will keep getting what you've been getting; it's that simple. Start breaking your old routines and rituals, meet new friends, travel, and meet new people. If you want to fly with the eagles, you must stop surrounding yourself with chickens; otherwise, you will never get off the ground. You have to be a different person. If you change, your circumstances will change.

When I started to adopt a new mindset, to invest in

books, to read one book a week, in a couple of months, my life changed. I was different. I retooled myself with the books. I decided to quit the job I had for ten years. I wanted more out of life because I believed I could get more. I have invested in coaching to help me to show me the way to success. Go ahead and get out of your comfort zone. Comfort kills dreams. Don't get locked up in your own prison. It's a beautiful life with so much to do, discover, and experience. FREE YOURSELF

Chapter 7

Push your limits

My wife and I were delighted when we finally found a two-bedroom apartment in a brand-new building in Long Island, NY, that we liked. I remember building a bookshelf in one of my spare rooms and immersing myself in reading biographies of successful entrepreneurs. I became a voracious reader, devoting long hours every day to my books. However, after two years in the apartment, I felt the need for something more. My standards had outgrown my current living situation, and I desired to express more of myself.

One day while jogging, we stumbled upon an apartment building with a gym, clean pool, grill area, large club room for tenants, and various other amenities. I suggested that we schedule a tour, and my wife agreed.

After finishing our jog, I engaged in a conversation with the superintendent, some of my neighbors, and myself. I was sharing with them about a new building I had come across. The superintendent warned me, saying, "Living in that building is like taking on a large mortgage. I would advise you to stay here." He also mentioned that he had a tenant who had moved in a year ago but had quickly moved out after only a few months. His words left me feeling discouraged and with a headache. Despite his warning, I decided to ignore his advice and show the building to my wife.

During our tour of the complex, we were impressed by the variety of amenities. We had a productive meeting with management, and when asked about our move-in plans, I confidently shared that we were ready to move in immediately. My wife expressed concern about our finances, but I reminded her that we didn't need a down payment and would be just fine. Seven years later, we're still happily residing in the complex and have no regrets about taking that initial step of faith. Initially, we faced some financial challenges, but we have since been able to keep up with expenses comfortably. In fact, it's so effortless that we now have our sights set on conquering new heights.

My mom told me one day that when you ask God for a penny, God won't give you more than a penny. You get what you expect, no more than that. I was expecting to pay the rent every month, and I always did, regardless it was $1000 or $10,000. When you tell your mind that this is the new standard now, your mind will help you find a way to keep that standard. If you see a beautiful house and say to yourself, "I will never be able to afford this kind of home, your mind will go to work to prove to you that you are right. It will build a good case for why you should not entertain that idea by bringing past failures, misfortunes, or experiences where you came up short.

Over the years, our minds can become deeply attached to a myriad of fixed ideas. It's ironic that these ideas that we cling to actually bind us to be a limited person make our life heavy, and rob us of our natural happiness.

I can't afford this; I'm too tired, I can't go to the gym, I'm not smart enough, and I don't have time. It's an escape for some people, it's too easy to say that. It's a statement, and a statement closes the mind, but a question will open the mind; instead of saying I can't afford it, ask yourself how can I afford it? And if you are really serious about it, your mind will work days and nights to find ways to make it happen. That's how life is. You should constantly re-evaluate all areas of your life and raise the standards. There is always room for growth. No matter who you are, you can always do better.

Also, it would be best if you only had quality people in your circle of friends. When you meet new people, try to talk about your big ideas, like buying a mansion or a jet, taking trips overseas, doing big things, and listening to their responses. If they're shooting you down if they tell you that you should take it easy and to save your money or be careful, stop wasting any more time with them. Their limited thinking will pollute your mind. Try to limit your association with them if you can. In his book The Measure of A Man, Sidney Poitier said, "When you go for a walk with someone, something happens unconsciously, it's not spoken, either you adjust to their space, or they adjust to your space." Whose space have you been adjusting to?

Some people's standard of living is only to be able to pay the rent, and most of the time, they do. It does not matter how bad the economy is. Even if they lose their jobs, they always find a way to pay the rent because that's their standard of living. If you want to know what it is going to take to get things to a higher level, to change your business or your life permanently, not temporarily, you have to raise your standards. If you are the smartest one in your group, you need a new group.

Raising standards is the only thing that creates lasting change and brings you a better life personally and professionally. You can lose weight all you want, but if you don't raise your standards on your eating habits, diet, and exercise, all that weight will come back.

Define the new standard. Instead of saying to yourself, "I want to lose 30 pounds", say to yourself, "I want to get back to my natural weight. I want to be fit and muscular." Go cut up a picture of a fit person from a magazine and photoshop it by cutting off their head and putting yours in there. Put this picture up somewhere that you can see every day. Your mind will have a hard time believing that this is the new standard initially because it's uncomfortable, different, and not what you are used to. Your routines will change, of course, and the mind doesn't like any change. It loves to be on autopilot. But remember, anything worthwhile is hard at first. It also takes 30 days to form a new habit. So, keep forcing yourself to believe your new standard until your mind accepts it.

When we decided to move to our new place, it was not easy initially. We struggled to keep up with the expenses, the rent payment was three times what we used to pay, but we decided that this was our new standard, so we had to find ways to afford this new lifestyle. Guess what we did; now it's the new normal but don't rest on your laurels, keep climbing, keep raising them, and don't concern yourself with the outside circumstances, recession, and Covid-19 to stop you from raising your standard.

A friend of mine decided to move to Alabama from New York a few years back to find a better place and cheaper rent because living in New York is very expensive. He tried to convince me for months to come with him, but I told him, "No." I don't really want to go where things are easier and cheaper because that's the wrong place to be. That's the bottom of the pyramid where a majority of people live. If the situation does not challenge you, it won't change you. You get what you paid for. It's not the environment or things that became so expensive all of a sudden. The real problem is you. You need to raise your standards. Anything is possible for you. The Bible said, "Ask, and it shall be given to you: seek, and you will find; knock, and it shall be opened unto you. " If one can do something great, so can you.

Raising your standard requires new thinking. You got to feed your mind with new ideas, a new discipline, new work ethic. New perspective drives new performance. You got to invest time in reading books because that's where life-changing ideas reside. Someone said if you want to hide something from black folks, put it in a book. They will never find it. Reading a book is a nightmare for some people. However, reading is to the mind what exercise is to the body. If you want to get your mind strong, invest in books. Phil Knight shares in his book how he built Nike starting with $50. Howard Schultz has a book on how he started Starbucks. Countless other billionaires share their stories in their books. The information is free to use all over the internet. If you don't like to read, go on YouTube or audible, and someone will read it to you while you are exercising or driving to work. You have to participate in your own rescue. It would help if you had new thinking to replace the old thinking machine. The thought that brought you here won't get you out. Invest part of your income in you to build a better you, smarter, stronger, wiser, better earner. Be intentional about it because you are your greatest asset. Build the library in the house, and kids will read too when they see daddy or mommy reading. You can achieve more than what you're doing right now.

Pick the best area in town you would love to live in and start brainstorming how you can make it happen; give yourself a chance, and believe for a moment that it is possible for you and that you deserve it. Try to do hard things, be unrealistic with yourself, and aim higher; as Earl Nightingale said, you become what you think about. Whatever is going on between your two ears becomes your reality. If you are fearful, doubting yourself all the time, and living in the past, you will manifest that in your life. That's why it's crucial to stand guard at the door of your mind, don't let your past failures pollute your thinking.

My friend Henock said to me one day, "Bro, don't you know that the world is ruled by C students? You really don't need to be intelligent, smart, or of a certain height or weight or have any obvious advantage to win in life." If you want to change your life, you have to approach life as a Lion. The lion is not the biggest, the largest, the fastest, tallest, smartest animal in the jungle, and yet he is the King of the Jungle. What makes the lion so unique? Why would a lion become the King of the Jungle when he has all those limitations? That's the million-dollar question. He's the King of the Jungle because of one word: ATTITUDE. The lion has a different attitude, and that makes every animal scared of him. The lion isn't taller than the giraffe, or bigger than the elephant, or heavier than the hippo, or smarter than the hyena or the snake, and yet when he shows up, they all run away. These larger and smarter animals respect such a small cat because of his attitude. The lion will see an elephant, and the thing that comes to his mind is lunch. The elephant is 50 times bigger than the lion, a hundred times heavier, and has more power. One stomp of his foot can destroy the lion.

But when the lion sees the elephant, he does not look at size, weight, or power. He's thinking of lunch. I can eat this thing. The lion acts the way he thinks, and size is not the problem. What makes the lion act is the way he thinks, and because he thinks that he can eat the elephant, he attacks him. He got that leadership attitude. Now here is another mystery: the elephant is bigger, larger, more powerful, heavier, and more intelligent. And yet, when the elephant sees the lion, one word comes to mind: Run. The elephant is controlled by the way he thinks. He thinks he's lunch. Therefore, his size, his weight, his power, and authority is a victims of the way that he thinks. It does not matter how big you are, how intelligent you are, or how many college degrees you have; it's your mind that keeps you small.

You're bigger than your circumstances. You can do anything. You can go from zero to a billion. The only thing stopping you is your mind, and that's where the fight is. Get rid of the limitations you set for yourself; change the identity you unconsciously gave yourself. Some people jump from a 50K job to another 50K job because they identify themselves unconsciously with being this 50K person. How do you iden- tify yourself? We live who we believe we are. I came across this quote that said, "sky is the limit." I believe that the sky is not the limit; the mind is.

Raise your standards, and turn your "Should" to "Must." Look at it this way: You usually do the things that you should do when it's comfortable and convenient and when it goes your way. But when you define something as a

Must, meaning you must do this or something bad is going to happen, guess what? You will find a way to get it done regardless of the circumstances.

My previous employer wanted to keep me as a technician because I was more valuable to them as a tech. However, I knew it was a dead-end job for me. I didn't want to become like some of my colleagues who started there before I was born. They were old-timers doing the same work for over 40 years. I had a different vision of my future for myself. My standards were higher than being a technician for all my life. The ideas those employers had about me were their ideas. I understood their angle, but I had a different angle for myself. My friend, the one who was trying to persuade me to move to Alabama with him, also had his own vision of my future. At that time, I was dealing with my shortcomings every day, and it made perfect sense to move with him. However, I didn't want to lower my standards, so I stayed in New York and dealt with the difficulties I faced. I love what motivational speaker Les Brown said: "We come in this world bold, naked, speechless, and dumb, everything else we learn." If someone can do something, so can you. When times are hard, don't retreat, don't back down. Where there is a will, there is a way. Raise your standards and live a better life because when you retreat or back down, trying to find an easier way, there is no growth to that; you won't gain anything.

I did not want to keep running like a gazelle in the jungle, always looking over my shoulder for what was coming next, living in fear every day that things might get worse.

Someone said that the world belongs to those who wake up early. I'm up at 4:30 am to read. That's the best time for me to read and write for the first 2 hours while everybody is sleeping and the house is quiet. When I am done reading, I go for my 45 min run, where I listen to my audiobooks and other inspirational speeches. I follow these rituals every day, regardless of rain or snow. I don't debate when it comes to my personal development. Be up early, show up to your commitments, get your day started early, and discipline yourself to get a strong morning ritual. How you start the day will define the day. You get rewarded in public for what you practice for years in private. And the Good Lord helps those who help themselves. I understood early on that when we are hard on ourselves, life becomes easy on us, but when we are easy on ourselves, life becomes hard on us.

When I decided to write this book, I wasn't intentional about it. I just wanted to write and publish a book so that I could get some bragging rights here and there. But it wasn't until I clearly defined my goals as a writer and speaker that I concluded that I must write this book. I used to write when I felt like writing and when I was inspired. It usually took me so long for me to get started. When I became intentional about my book, I scheduled writing on my calendar, and my Should became Must. Every day I wrote for two hours, and time flew by. I had to get this book going. I was writing in the car on the way to work after I finished repairing the bank ATMs while I was in traffic. I was writing throughout the day. I used to wait until I got home, showered, relaxed, and waited until everything was quiet for me to write. But then I learned that I had to force the situation and get myself comfortable with my discomfort. Whether I felt inspired or not, I had to write. That's when things changed. I wrote most of the book in my woodworking shop in the middle of the sawdust, miter box, saw, smoke, and all that. I wrote everywhere. I felt like I could bring the task anywhere and get it done, not wait for things to go my way to write.

Perfect time or perfect day does not exist, now is the perfect time to start, embrace the discomfort, and grow. When something is a must for you, it does not matter if it's comfortable or not. You will find a way to get it done.

If everybody around you is gaining a little weight and is constantly tired after some time while you have a high energy level, you don't want to tease them or make them feel bad. So gradually, subconsciously, you lower your own standards just a little bit. If you take a frog and dump him in hot water, it will jump right out. But if you put him in warm water and turn up the heat really slowly, over time, it will boil to death. That's most people's lives. You have to understand the power of association.

Some people think they're like trees, and there is nothing they can do to change their situation. They stay in jobs they hate because it's familiar, it's easy. Wanting more requires getting out of your comfort zone and taking risks. Hating your job should be motivating enough to raise your standard to find one that you like, which is more flexible and more money. For things to get better, you must be better. It's an internal switch that you flip on by going to work on yourself. Author Jim Rohm said, "You need to work harder on yourself than your job." When you invest time in growing yourself, you will make a fortune; but your job will just pay your living; that's it. Excuses are just an indicator of your priorities. There is always time to do what you must do. Participate in your own rescue." Crying and whining are not going to help your situation; raise your standards instead.

One guy told me that he owed too much money and his goal was to get out of debt. However, the goal can't be just to get out of debt because that's how you remain in debt forever. The thinking has to be bigger than your present circumstances; otherwise, the same struggle will remain. You will be fighting the same problems. In the middle of the chaos, that's where you should raise the standards. Set goals to make ten times what you owe; don't just get out of debt.

Life is about getting better every day; success is not something you own or buy and put in your pocket, it's the rent you have to pay, and the due date is every day. You have to live successfully one day at a time. Put the focus on today, do the best you can today, just today that's the only thing you have. Do the best you can with what you have now. Like the bricklayer, one brick at a time. A strong work ethic will beat talent any day of the week.

The work-life balance nonsense doesn't exist for me. My wife loves me very much; she tells me to relax, slow down, chill, and enjoy life. She thinks that I might burn out.

But you don't slow down or relax from doing what you love or fighting for your life; you want to keep doing it. Tell that to the gazelle in the middle of the jungle full of lions. The gazelle is not about to slow down. He's trying to outrun the slowest gazelle; if not, he's dead.

Henry Ford was the founder of the Ford Motor Company, and if we count his net worth in today's money, he would be worth $188 billion. Henry Ford strongly believed in a life full of hard work and not a life of ease. There's an interesting story from his days when Ford Motor Company was already a profitable and prosperous company at that time, and Ford was making around 100 cars per day. Henry Ford then announced that he planned to make 1000 cars per day, now some of the stockholders of his company were alarmed and shocked; they were happy and satisfied with the profits Ford was making, and they did not want to see the company go through the pains of growing and adopting new technology to get 1000 cars per day. They thought that Henry Ford was going to ruin the company by trying to increase production, and they even threatened him with lawsuits. Henry Ford said the end of money is not eased; instead, it should be used to perform more service he believed in working hard for the sake of building something great rather than for the sake of making money so that you can retire and live a life of ease he goes on to say nothing is more abhorrent than a life of ease. None of us has any right to ease. There is no place in civilization for the idler he strongly believed that if you focus on doing great work and providing great service, you will have more money than you can ever spend. He hated the idea that some people just wanted to get to a life of ease. Life is not a battle that should be ended as soon as possible.

Success, by definition, lies beyond the realm of normal action. Being realistic equals being average, and nobody wants to live an average life. You must be unrealistic to be successful, set your goals higher, and don't play small when it comes to you. I personally know people who want to be successful with great ideas, but they come up short on the amount of action required to get their lives to the exceptional level they deserve. Massive action is the key. Upgrade your thinking, shoot for the top, the bottom is crowded.

Chapter 8

Tough Times don't last

A farmer had an old donkey. One night the donkey fell into the well. The farmer heard the noise coming from the well and discovered the difficult situation that the donkey put himself into. The farmer assessed the situation, and though he felt sympathy for the donkey, he decided that neither the old donkey nor the well was worth the trouble of saving. Instead, he called his two sons and asked them to help him haul dirt to bury the poor animal in the well and put it out of its misery.

At first, when the donkey felt all this dirt hitting on his head, he got panicky. But as the three men continued shoveling, a smart idea struck him. Every time a shovel of dirt landed on his back, he would shake it off and step up! And this is what he continued to do! He would shake the dirt off and step up! Shake the dirt off and step up! He kept saying these words out loud to encourage himself. "Shake it off and step up! Shake it off and step up!"

Every blow was painful, and the situation seemed terrible, but the donkey tried to stay focused, to fight the panic, and to keep shaking the dirt off and stepping up. After a while, the exhausted donkey managed to step over the wall of the well. What a relief! The dirt that seemed like it would have buried him alive actually helped him to survive. The donkey handled his adversity in the best possible way.

When you face severe challenges, your mind is at its sharpest; it kicks in and thinks beyond the norms. Tony Robbins said it so eloquently: "Life happens for you, not to you." I think if you understand that, it's a game-changer. Things happen in your life to enhance and make you better and stronger. There is always a reason why something happened to you.

In his book The Obstacle is the way, Ryan Holiday said that instead of looking at your problems as obstacles to stop you in your tracks, look at them as challenges. The Obstacle is the way. When going through hell, keep going; in the end, you will prevail. Don't always try to find the easy way out because every challenge has opportunities lying underneath. Looking at your life and the problems or challenges you had growing up, some of them helped you become the person you are today and built your character. If you face your issues not as problems but as challenges and stepping stones to your destination, and refuse in the process to give in to panic, fear, and anxiety, then you can focus on finding a way to tackle the issue. How you react to challenges is very important. As Charles R. Swindoll said, "Life is 10% what happens to you and 90% how you react to it." So, you are in charge.

The 13th-century Persian poet Rumi said, "The wound is the place where light enters you." This quote is so profound. There is no single thing that has ever happened to you or will happen to you that will be wasted. Confronting every crisis, difficulty, or challenge in your life or the world will make you more of who you are meant to be. Awareness of your pain is your opportunity to let the light in you. That's where the learning starts. Sometimes in life, you encounter painful lessons you will never forget.

You'll never learn much if everything goes as planned, you get what you want, things are working in your favor, you win all the time, and you have no challenges. You won't grow much that way, and that's boring. Challenges are necessary.

Nelson Mandela was in "the hole" for 27 years. He often said that suffering builds character, character breeds faith, and, in the end, faith will not disappoint. Mandela entered prison as a violent revolutionary and emerged as a nonviolent peacemaker and reconciler. Prison turned him into a realist, aware of the difficulty of healing the racial wounds in South Africa. He dug himself out by studying, being patient, and staying strong to become the fourth president of South Africa.

They have something they call the Chinese bamboo tree in the Far East. The Chinese bamboo takes three to five years to grow. As they go through the process of growing it, they have to water and fertilize the ground every day. The tree does not break through the ground until the fifth year. But once it does, it grows to 90 feet tall within five weeks. Does it grow 90 feet tall in five weeks or five years? The answer is obvious – it grows 90 feet tall in five years because if they had stopped nurturing, watering, and fertilizing that seed within those five years, the bamboo tree would have died in the ground.

It takes time to be successful. It's not a 100-meter dash sprint; it's a marathon. It takes time to achieve anything worthwhile, and there is no such thing as overnight success. It was embarrassing when I returned from Africa after failing big time to start a business there. My friend trusted me with his money to do well in business for us, but I came back with a huge amount of debt. I had to restart again with a low-paying job that I hated. I knew it was beneath me to be doing that kind of work. I was working there with people that I was old enough to be their father. I did not want to tell them how old I was. I made sure I shaved every day for them so they would not see my gray hair. To stop the bleeding, I needed to get some money coming in ASAP. It was hard for me to face my friend and not be able to pay him his money back after I persuaded him to invest in me so that we could make some money together.

Here is what I learned at that stage: Things will happen to you, and you will go through your obstacles and setbacks without understanding why you had to go through this humiliating, painful process. You'll wonder why this is happening to you, but after you go through them, after the storm is over, you will realize why you had to go through it, why you needed that lesson. It was meant to prepare you for bigger and better things. That pain forced me to start a new business, take on another job, save money, and invest in stocks. I used to count the days until payday, but it's not the case anymore. Life is made of challenges. Welcome them, don't run from them. Step toward them, don't try to duck or avoid them as most people do. Remember: Adversity introduces a man to himself. Most people want it easy, but easy come, easy go.

Henry Ford said, "When everything seems to be going against you, remember that the airplane takes off against the wind, not with it." A Delta Airlines Pilot told me the same thing a few years back when I was flying to Guangzhou, China; he said the only time the aircraft uses all its power is during take-off, and once it reaches the right altitude, the autopilot mode kicks in. Every beginning is hard; Tough times never last; only tough people do, as Robert

Schuller puts it. You will go through setbacks and difficulties to achieve something meaningful. Nothing will be given to you. Nope, success is not going to land on your lap. You have to work on it to get that dream or business.

However, you don't need to take this journey completely alone. I learned from Daymond John, the creator of FUBU (For Us, By Us) and founder of The Shark Tank consulting, that being an entrepreneur is a team sport – you can't be successful by yourself, you're not an Island, you need other people to help you, not just in business, in your personal life too, don't feel ashamed or embarrassed when you need help. Get a Life coach, a mentor, or books to help you personally or professionally. You have to find a way to leverage people. Nowadays, with technology, you can easily leverage people across the world. When I was writing this book, I needed to do some research online. I hired a few freelancers online to help me, people more knowledgeable than me on that subject. You have to surround yourself with people who can help you.

If you have a task to do and know that it is something you know very little about or don't want to spend your valuable time on a task that someone else can do for you, delegate it. I used to hire lots of freelancers from oDesk.com and Fiverr.com, and so on. You can find people worldwide, the very best at what they do, for dirt cheap. I could not afford to hire people in the U.S.A. for my work project, but I could find someone overseas, in China, Bangladesh, or India, who is best at what they do, affordable. I remember I had a personal assistant I hired from Fiveer; she lives in India and is a brilliant lady, she asked me for $4/hr, and I had to give her more; she was very productive and helped me make my work effortless. Big difference in time zones between U.S. and India. While I was sleeping, she was working. I was getting things done around the clock. She checked in when I checked out at night. I would give her assignments once I got up early in the morning. She had the work done. Leveraging other people's time is very useful. Big U.S. corporations do it all the time. Before hiring someone, they must go through a process to see if a machine, automated, or software program can do the task. If not, they check overseas to see if they could hire someone outside the U.S., which is much cheaper. If not, then they consider hiring someone locally. Their mindset is to do whatever it takes to stretch their money. You have to operate the same way.

Think about that as you are trying to grow your business or working on your idea. Hire people through freelancing for a week or two, and test them to see if they can help you. It would help if you had a team around you to help you achieve your goals faster. Get a coach to keep you on your toes if you can. That's teamwork, and you will pull more quickly with a team.

There is no free lunch unless you were born with a silver spoon in your mouth, and everything is done for you. I would hate that, just my opinion, because you'll never know what it takes to build or accomplish anything. When everything is handed to you, you won't value anything. But when you work your tail off to build a company from the ground up, from nothing, that's more rewarding to me.

Life has its down periods:
Your boss is unhappy with you.
Your business is struggling.
You get into a fight with the love of your life.
Your finances are tight.
You aren't getting a good night's sleep.
You get sick or have chronic pain.
Our way of dealing with this is usually to do one or more of the following:

Get away from the problem — quit your job, break up with your partner, stop caring, or do anything else you can do to exit. Ignore the problem — don't think about it. Pretend nothing's wrong.
Comfort ourselves — drink, smoke, food, T.V., Internet, porn, social media, games, or something similar to take our minds off the difficulties.
Complain — lash out at someone, rant, moan about it to a friend. Feel resentful. Tell yourself that the other person is the problem.

There's nothing wrong with any of these things. Don't feel guilty if you do them. Sometimes, they can be soothing or helpful. For example, talking to someone about your problems is a good idea. Giving yourself rest so that you are better prepared to tackle the world's problems is not bad. But trying to avoid the problem, exit from it, or even comfort yourself has limited effectiveness. You know that because the downtimes keep happening despite your best efforts. You get in a slump, you get miserable, and you feel down.

Here's a mental shift that might help when you're feeling hurt, sad, angry, or overburdened. Think of it not as a problem but as an experience. Fully feel whatever pain or sadness, or anger you're feeling. Stop avoiding it and just feel it. Truly allow yourself to feel it. And as you feel it, don't think of the difficult feeling as a problem you need to solve or a thing you need to get rid of. Think of it as an experience you're having – it's always an experience that shall pass. Tough times never last.

Ralph Waldo Emerson said, "All life is an experiment. The more experiments you make, the better." Quit wanting to own things all the time. Spend time alone with yourself and experience your fear, challenges, victories, and shortcomings with a calm mindset. Nothing lasts for a lifetime, even life is temporary.

Chapter 9

Declutter

The Mrs. picked out the smallest closet in our first two-bedroom apartment in Long island and said, "This will be your closet." My first reaction was, "What?! Are you kidding? Why should mine be the smallest one out of the four? That's not fair! She says, "Oh, I have a lot more stuff; a lady needs room in the house ." I knew she had more stuff than me. In 5 min tops, you can move all my stuff out of the house. I only have a few things. My wife had clothes and shoes in bins that she had kept for years. We previously had a big walk-in closet, which I called the squeeze-in closet because I had to squeeze in there to find stuff. It was ridiculous. She owns lots of clothes, beautiful ones taking space in the closets without being used. Every time I open her closet, my head hurts. She does not wear them or give them away; my mom does the same thing. It must be a female thing. Women love options. I guess they just want to see the closet full of clothes and feel good about owning stuff.

I own very few outfits so as not to clutter my space. Less is always better for me. She usually takes way too long to get dressed. She has to try on three or four dresses before making a choice. Having too many choices seems very unproductive and a waste of time. President Obama said that he only had two colors of suits, gray and black. Today it's gray; tomorrow, it's black. He doesn't waste brain power to think about what he's going to wear.

If you see someone living in a cluttered environment, it really means that that person is not fully invested. He or she is not reaching their full potential.

Did you know that people with a messy workspace are less efficient and more frustrated than those who have an organized work desk? Well, now you do! So don't put it off until tomorrow; declutter your workspace ASAP. You can start by getting rid of all the non-essential items and assigning a proper place to everything. The best way to keep things organized without feeling overwhelmed or exhausted is to clean up your work desk every day before you go home. A Branch manager at Chase Bank, the largest bank in the USA, said to me that when you perform your work in an area free of clutter, when you only have the one thing you are working on in front of you, you are more focused, your mind won't be distracted, and, as a result, you are more effective. That's why every time I used to go to service that bank's machine after hours, all the desks were cleaned and organized. It is a must for employees to keep their work areas clean and free of clutter.

We recently got rid of our big entertainment center, which cleared out a big space in our living room. We bought a much smaller one and hung the TV on the wall. My wife said to me, "Oh, look! Now we have a lot of empty spaces. What are we going to do about it?" "Nothing," I said, "Nothing at all. Let it be free! There's no need to fill that space. This is a home, not a storage locker!" Because clutter is the ultimate disease, I have new rules in the house. If something is not used for 30 days, we got two options, sell it or donate it.

We can declutter not only our physical space but also our mind. But let's first talk about the physical clutter, from our cell phones to our homes and everything in between.

My phone used to beep frequently because of the stupid notifications that kept stealing my focus when I was working on a project. I was getting tired of being interrupted to check my phone. I blamed myself for downloading all the apps I found in entrepreneurial magazines and thinking they could help me be more productive. I was dead wrong. One day for some very strange reason, I reset my phone to factory default, and the apps were gone. I thought I had made the worst possible mistake; my phone was emptied, with nothing in it. I was nervously shocked. However, a few days later, I was glad I did because I was spending less time on the phone and more time working. Now I'm more productive and more focused on getting my job done. By accidentally decluttering my phone, I have realized that our phones can take a big chunk of our time, focus, and energy. Sometimes it's another life we are living through our phones. I often see people at different places glued to their phones, busy being busy but doing basically nothing.

What gets scheduled gets done. So, I schedule 15 minutes a day on my calendar to declutter my place. I believe in my calendar. Today I was in my closet, questioning everything, every item. I checked my clothes, socks, underwear, suits, shirts, and so on to make sure that I was utilizing those items. If I find a shirt I don't like to wear anymore, and it's a good-looking shirt, I donate it and get rid of it. I want to have only clothes that I feel good wearing.

Every day I get rid of five things I don't need for the next 30 days to make room either on my phone, in my house, in my car, or in my shop. Find five things to take out of the house, give them to a charity, sell them, or donate them. Whatever you do, make sure that you won't see those things again. Don't get rid of something and then buy the same thing again – it defeats the purpose. You do that for 30 days and see what happens to your life. First of all, you will be more aware of the things that you bring into the house. Your eyes will be scanning every day for things that you don't need. Your living space has to be free of clutter. Just furnish your space with the things that you need, not the things that

you want, because the latter are the things that will most likely eat up all of your money.

There are things that are cool to have in the house, don't
get me wrong. There are certain things that I love to have at
my place. The problem I have is that people use their credit
cards to buy something that they want, but those things will
lose value before the bill is paid in full –costing them more.
You have to be aware of that. I'd rather use that money to
go on trips and to experience another country than spend
my money on things that lose value so quickly. Forget about
owning things – go experience life.

We talked about the physical clutter, but there is also
mental clutter, and it's even worse. I schedule the same 15
minutes a day to declutter my mind also. I meditate a lot.
Ideas that I'm pursuing, projects, my commitments, workout, personal development, family, and time off. I'm trying
to fine-tune my thinking, staying focused on a few projects
instead of many. Meditating on an upcoming day helps me
stay focused, clear my thinking, and set goals. Things that
you said you were going to do today – maybe fix the floor
or build a wall in the back – those things will be cluttering
your mind if you don't do them. You create mental clutter by
procrastinating. Of course, you say to yourself that you will
get this thing done by tomorrow, but tomorrow comes, and
you put it off again. Every time you look at that stuff, it will
stare back at you, and you won't feel good about that. If you
do that every day and let stuff accumulate for a few years,
you will feel like a total loser. You won't trust yourself, and

that will lower your self-confidence, and your self-worth will diminish. Keep promises you made to yourself. Finish what you started. Get it done.

Professional organizer Scott Roewer has rightly put it this way: "Clutter is simply delayed decisions." When you constantly put off making decisions, your brain becomes overwhelmed by all those pending decisions that's created. So, stop procrastinating and make that call, whether it's the email, or the work you've been avoiding to do for so long.

Talking to a loved one about how you feel is a great way to release pent-up emotions. Sharing your thoughts with others can also help you look at things from a fresh perspective and, as a result, think clearer and make better decisions.

Former USA President Abraham Lincoln had a friend he usually called to the White House to speak to him. Most of the time, his friend didn't even say a word. Lincoln was doing all the talking because he just wanted to unload, he wanted to hear himself talk, and it was super productive for him. His friend was not a psychologist or a therapist; he was there to listen to the President working on strategies for running the country

Journaling is a great way to relax your mind by analyzing and organizing your thoughts. According to research published in the "Journal of Experimental Psychology," general, expressive writing eliminates intrusive thoughts about negative events and improves working memory. Researchers believe that these improvements may, in turn, free up our cognitive resources for other mental activities, including the ability to manage stress more effectively. A University of Rochester Medical Center report states that writing in a daily journal can also help manage anxiety and cope with depression, as it's a healthy outlet to release bottled emotions. You don't have to be a prolific writer to start a journal. For beginners, bullet journaling is one of the easiest techniques to try out.

We live in a world of stresses and worries, errands, projects, and noise that we must all endure. All of it inflicts upon our mind clutter and chaos and leaves us with a mind that sometimes cannot find calmness. Because we desperately need that headspace to be able to focus and make the best decisions, we feel angry and upset without it. It's similar to unsuccessfully trying to find something you need for a work project among numerous papers, mail, correspondence, magazines, and paperwork on your desk. So frustrating! Over-scheduling and multitasking won't get you anywhere. You will be stuck constantly looking for the things you need to accomplish your goals and not being able to notice them. We spend hours online: reading blogs, managing Pinterest boards, watching viral videos on YouTube, etc. That abundance of information can clog your brain, causing stress and anxiety.

I read a while back an old Japanese parable. One day someone came to an old and wise Japanese man to ask for advice because his life was so stressful. He was working so hard, but he did not feel like he was getting anywhere. So, the old man invited him to his house to have a cup of tea. They sat down and got comfortable as the old man poured tea into the cups. He filled his cup first with less than half of the cup, then started to fill his guest's cup. He kept filling the cup, but the tea was overflowing. His guest asked, "What are you doing? Don't you see the cup is overflowing? Stop! This is insane. Are you OK?" The old man said to him, "This is what you are doing to yourself. You can get a bigger cup to fill in more tea, but you can't get another mind to fill in with more stuff. You must reduce the intake."

Take some time for yourself! Make sure to schedule breaks throughout the day where you can disconnect from your devices and just be with your thoughts. Your brain deserves a break to recharge and operate at its best. Have some fun too! Do something that brings you joy, like taking a nap or going for a walk in the park. Personally, I love spending time in my shop working with my hands on projects like drawing and building things. Right now, I'm even creating a plastic shredding machine to recycle plastic!

Sticking to a daily routine is crucial! I make sure to follow my routine every day, no matter how I'm feeling. It's become a habit, just like brushing my teeth - I don't even have to think about it anymore. One of my favorite parts of my routine is my daily 5-mile run. As soon as I wake up, I say a prayer, lace up my shoes, and hit the pavement. I do it at the same time every day, and it gives me a sense of accomplishment and control for the rest of the day.

Unwinding is great – take some time off. You can't see

the frame when you are in the picture. I get myself out of the frame by traveling abroad. Sometimes I just shut everything down and leave the country to expose myself to unknown places that I have never been – see different people, embrace cultures, eat different foods, and talk to strangers – these things make me forget about myself. It also helps me to create some headspace.

What if I told you that you also could declutter your life and make more room for what truly matters? Less clutter, more organization. Less stress, more time. Less debt, more freedom. Less discontent, more intention. So how do you declutter a mind? Someone said that the mind is a terrible thing to waste, and it's better to invest in it. It's the battleground; everything is in the mind; it's a mental world we're living in right now. The difference between the poor and the rich lies in how they use their minds. Pick an area of your life you want to improve – financial, health, career, relationship with your spouse or spiritual creator – and follow the four steps below to make positive changes in it.

First Step: Decide on that area specifically as possible; you might say, "Well, I'm 28 pounds overweight," or "I wake up exhausted in the morning," or "I want to earn more money, improve my finances," or "I'm not in a relationship, and I want to be intimate with someone," or "I'm in a relationship, and I wish I weren't, so I'm planning my escape," or whatever. Then you write down the truth about where you are right now in that matter so that you're really clear about it. Be very specific about that area.

The Second Step: Be really honest with yourself. There are some rituals that are bringing you your current results Rituals are something you do every day, a series of actions, or a type of behavior that you follow consistently. There are some rituals of what you eat or don't eat or how you move or don't move, and what you do or don't do. There's a lack of variety, energy, or focus in some areas that are bothering you. There's something you're doing – it's usually not one thing; it's a bunch of little things you do consistently. Whenever you think about getting into a relationship or about, working out, or about money or whatever, you get yourself into a state of feeling overwhelmed. You start thinking about things you can't control. If you ask yourself why you're overweight, why you can't seem to lose any weight, it's because you have rituals that keep you there, bad eating habits, wrong selection of food, no proper rest, and no workout. It's a series of little things that you do every day while thinking it doesn't matter. Everything affects everything else.

Tony Robbins said that success or failure is not a giant event that shows up one day in your life. It's a bunch of little things that you do consciously or unconsciously every day. Some people are in a vicious cycle. They keep doing the same thing day in and day out, getting the same results and wondering why they're not getting ahead, why they're still broke. Being broke is a state of mind. You can get out of it anytime you want. There are rituals, a bunch of little things that you do in that area that keep you there, nothing else. So, write down all the rituals you have.

The Third Step: What do you want? What's your vision in that area? Be really specific in describing your vision.

The Fourth Step: What are the rituals that will get you there? What would you do differently each day? If you're going to have that kind of energy and that kind of strength, when would you schedule your workout? It would be best if you did something consistently at a specific time so it becomes automatic. Willpower doesn't last, but rituals last a lifetime. I bet you have some rituals in your life right now that you've been doing for years, even though some of them don't serve you well at all. I'm just saying to wake yourself up.

Change is always a matter of motivation, never a matter of ability. And that motivation stems from a strong reason, a burning desire, a drive. If you have a strong desire to do something, you will find a way to do it. You make the decision to do something, then the "how" will unfold as you go.

I used to get overwhelmed when it came to changing bad habits in my life because I was asking myself the wrong questions: How can I change? How can I improve my health, my decision-making, and my finances? Jim Rohm says, "Don't ask HOW; ask WHY." Why should you change? Why should you improve your health? The Why will give you the reason to change, to be, or do better in any area of your life—a strong WHY leads to a Strong Result.

Outsmart yourself, declutter your life, and create a clutter-free life, physical and mental. Take time and empty your mind into a journal. People nowadays don't carry pens anymore; everything is done digitally on the phone or computer. I love pens so much that I make my own pens. The act of writing in a journal for 20 to 30 minutes every day is therapy for me. I have my own corner in the house, which is on the toilet seat. I love my bathroom. I am in the process of building a bookshelf in the bathroom, don't tell my wife (hahaha).

On a cold January morning, a man sat at a metro station in Washington DC, and started to play the violin. He played six Bach pieces for about 45 minutes. During that time, since it was rush hour, it was calculated that thousands of people went through the station, most of them on their way to work.

Three minutes went by, and a middle-aged man noticed there was a musician playing. He slowed his pace and stopped for a few seconds, and then hurried up to meet his schedule. A minute later, the violinist received his first dollar tip: a woman threw the money in his till and, without stopping, continued to walk. A few minutes later, a man leaned against the wall to listen to him but then looked at his watch and started to walk again. Clearly, he was late for work. The one who paid the most attention was a three-year-old boy. His mother tried to hurry him along, but the kid stopped to look and listen to the violinist. Finally, the mother pushed hard, and the child continued to walk, but he was turning his head all the time. This action was repeated by several other children. All the parents, without exception, forced them to move on. In the 45 minutes the musician played, only six people stopped and stayed for a while. About 20 gave him money, but he continued to walk at a normal pace. He collected $32. When he finished playing, and silence took over, no one noticed it. No one applauded, nor was there any recognition.

No one knew this, but the violinist was Joshua Bell, one of the best musicians in the world. He played one of the most intricate pieces ever written on a violin worth $3.5 million. Two days before his playing in the subway, Joshua Bell sold out at a theater in Boston, and the seats averaged $200.

This is a real story. Joshua Bell playing incognito in the metro station, was organized by the Washington Post as part of a social experiment about the perception, tastes, and priorities of people. The outlines were: in a commonplace environment at an inappropriate hour, do we perceive beauty? Do we stop to appreciate it? Do we recognize talent in an unexpected context?

Time flies, life moves so fast, and years and weeks go by so fast that you don't even remember what you did last week. Way too much stuff is thrown at you daily, clouding your focus. One of the possible conclusions from this experience could be: If we do not have a moment to stop and listen to one of the best musicians in the world playing the best music ever written, how many other things are we missing?

Slow down and smell your roses.

So, the biggest part of decluttering your life is knowing

what you want and having enough reason to follow through. Excessive clutter is often a symptom and a cause of stress and can affect every facet of your life – from the time it takes you to do things to your finances and your overall enjoyment of life. Clutter can distract you, weigh you down, and in general, invite chaos into your life.

Tackling the clutter can seem an insurmountable task if you don't know where or how to start. The best way to declutter your home, workspace, and life is to take things one small step at a time. Combined small steps will lead to big improvements that will be easier to maintain over the long run.

By devoting a little of your time to getting rid of the clutter in your life and maintaining things relatively clutter-free, you'll reap the rewards of pleasant living areas, reduced stress, and a more organized and productive existence.

Chapter 10

Less is better

At the time of his death, Steve Jobs, founder of Apple, had a Net worth of around $10 billion. There's a very interesting story from Jobs' life that crystallizes one of the biggest reasons behind his massive success. Many people do not know that Steve Jobs was fired as the CEO of Apple in 1985. He was fired from the company he founded. In the absence of Steve Jobs, Apple began to struggle and was very close to bankruptcy in the mid-90s. In the final quarter of 1996, Apple sales had plummeted by 30%, and it was struggling mightily. Steve Jobs was brought back to Apple as a CEO in 1997, and that is when he started the historical turnaround of Apple. Steve Jobs found out that the company had a line of 12 Macintosh computers just to satisfy retailers.

However, when he asked his top management which of these computers he should recommend to his friends, he needed help to get a clear answer. So, he got to work reducing the number of Apple products by 70%, and the company went from losing $1 billion that year to turning a profit of 309 million dollars a year later. He continued to stay focused and took Apple from the brink of bankruptcy in 1996 to one of the largest companies in the world in 2011 when he died. That is the power of focus. Apple grew because it cut down on things it focused on. Steve Jobs often said deciding what not to do is just as important as deciding what to do. This idea is true for companies, and it is true for products. Google co-founder Larry Page approached Steve Jobs for advice in his dying days. Here's what Job said: figure out what Google wants to be when it grows up, and don't be all over the place.

Simplicity is the art of focusing only on what's essential to your goals and your satisfaction and ignoring the rest. Instead of paying attention to everything, simplicity is choosing to pay attention only to things that matter the most and ignoring the rest. It's easy to say, but to be honest with you, I'm trying hard to practice that as I'm writing this book. It's not easy because I see shiny objects all over the place, very fun things I like to do, business or projects to do,

At 18 years old, my dad wanted me to be a doctor. The hell with being a doctor; I hated doctors. Even to this day, the smell of rubbing alcohol drives me nuts and gives me nightmares. When I was younger, I had some weird disease,

I still don't know the name of it, but I'm glad it's gone. I had to take a shot every day at the clinic next door to us. I hated it because it was painful; there was no way around it. I understand that being a doctor is valued, as my dad always said, and there is lots of money and job security in it. However, I'm glad I made it to the USA to escape my dad's dream he had for me. I would have been one angry doctor just to please my dad. How many people are doing just that? Mom and Dad are practicing law, and everyone in the family has to be a lawyer. I know Doctors who left their practice to be a woodworker and countless other people living their parent's dreams. I would rather make 50K doing something I love than make 150K in a job I can't stand.

Herb Kelleher, CEO of Southwest Airlines, has consistently produced amazing financial results year after year. In an interview I watched online, he said he's all about trade-offs at Southwest. Rather than trying to fly everywhere, to every destination, Southwest had deliberately chosen to offer point-to-point flights. And instead of jacking up prices to cover meal costs like Delta, American Airlines, and other airlines, he decided not to offer any meals. And instead of assigning seats in advance, they would let people choose their seats, with no first class, only coach. Each one of those trade-offs wasn't made by default but by design to keep prices down. Herb was clear about what the company was − a low-cost airline, and what they were not. His trade-offs reflected as much. At first, Southwest was bombarded by critics, naysayers, and other people who could not believe that his approach could possibly be successful. Other airlines were laughing at him. Who in their right mind would want to fly an airline that traveled only to certain places and didn't serve meals, no matter how cheap the tickets were? And yet, after a few years, competitors took notice that Southwest was onto something. Southwest became very profitable.

Think of Warren Buffet, who famously said, "My investment philosophy borders on lethargy." What he meant by that was that his firm makes relatively few investments and keeps them for a long time. He decided early in his career that it would be impossible for him to make hundreds of right investment decisions, so he decided that he would make a few investments in businesses that he was absolutely sure of and bet heavily on them. He owes 90% of his wealth just to ten investments. In short, he makes big bets on the essential few investment opportunities and says no to the many merely good ones.

I used to own a sign shop out on Long Island, New York, in 2011. I was making all kinds of signs for my customers. I was the designer, the sign maker, the marketer, and the salesman, doing everything to get the business off the ground and; in the meantime, I was also involved in some other side hustles and expecting to make some profit. At one point, I was running three businesses and a full-time job as an engineer for NCR, spreading myself too thin and flying off in different directions. I worked like hell for years, expecting to see profits in my businesses. I was always asking myself, "Why is it so hard to make money?" I found the answer later on with Reverend Ike; he said: whatever you're chasing in life will stay away from you. In my case, I was chasing money, and money was nowhere to be found. I was too busy being busy, still broke. I had complained for years that the business was not working. Maybe I was on the wrong side of town, and I should move to another area.

My wife would always say to me, "The way you are working, you should be a millionaire by now." I was all about making money, so I would chase every opportunity I saw to make money. Even if it had nothing to do with the sign business, I was always thinking that the grass might be greener somewhere else. I stumbled on the book Essentialism by Greg McKeown at the library. He wrote, "Working hard is important, but more effort does not necessarily yield better results. Less is more, and that change my thinking. What not to do is as important as what to do. You can do anything, but you can't do everything.

Most of the successful entrepreneurs in the world were known for doing one thing, and once they became successful, they diversified their portfolios. They were not chasing the money. It was always a passion for most of them. It was something they wanted to bring to this world, a product or service, or a sport that they loved to play to become great at it. Money was never the end result for them, and it was the joy of doing what they loved. Someone said, "Do what you love, and the money will follow." It has always been more than one thing for me. I'm passionate about creating and making things, but I always find myself in too many things.

A few years ago, I asked myself an important question: "If I could start over, what would I focus on doing with my life?" I realized that spreading myself thin and being a jack of all trades wasn't getting me anywhere. So, I decided to dedicate all my time to one passion - helping others grow through education and motivation. I have a love for teaching, as it was something I lacked when growing up in Senegal. Having good mentors and teachers around you is crucial, but it was hard to find in Senegal. Most people there had to learn through trial and error, which takes a lot of time and can lead to costly mistakes.

When I started to write, I read book after book and went to seminars to see the best speakers like Tony Robbins, Les Brown, and so. I had to boil it down to one thing. I had to ask myself what I wanted to be known for. What is that one thing that I cared so deeply about? Do just that one thing and forget about the rest?

It's easy to get caught up in the demands of modern life – the world is constantly increasing in complexity and placing more and more demands on your attention. If you try to tackle everything that grabs your attention, you'll constantly find yourself stressed, overwhelmed, and burned out. As life goes on, I think we tend to forget our ability to choose the things we want for ourselves, and we learn to be helpless. Drip by drip, we allow our power to be taken away until we end up becoming a function of other people's choices, hiring us for jobs we don't want, and settling for less than we deserve. We take jobs just for the money, which is the worst way to make money. We become miserable because we're stuck on that job for years, dreading retirement, "One day I will retire and live happily after." That's an empty life. If you are in a job, waiting to retire, you are on the wrong path. Just recognize the power you have to choose and celebrate it. If you give that power away to others or permit organizations to choose for you, unless that's a choice you would make, you won't have a meaningful life.

Ferran Adrià, who's arguably the world's greatest chef. He led El Bulli to become the world's most famous restaurant. He epitomizes the principle of "less is better" in at least two ways. First, his specialty is reducing traditional dishes to their absolute essence and then reimagining them in ways people had never thought of before. Second, while El Bulli has somewhere in the range of two million requests for dinner reservations each year, it serves only 50 people per night, and they close up for six months of the year to spend the other six months fine-tuning and sharpening its skills. When business is slow in most restaurants, they add more items to the menu, invest more money, spread themselves too thin, work employees harder, and end up making no progress. El Bulli, on the other hand, tries to reduce the items on the menu and focus on the few vital things that the restaurant is known for.

Back in 1895, the Italian economist Vilfredo Pareto noticed that 80 percent of Italian land belonged to 20 percent of the country's population. The Pareto principle states that for many phenomena, 80 percent of the result comes from 20 percent of the effort. Pareto surveyed other countries only to discover that the wealth was distributed more or less in similar disproportions everywhere. In business, a goal of the 80/20 rule is to identify inputs that are potentially the most productive and make them the priority. Instead of spreading yourself too thin, focusing on the essentials helps you accomplish the things that matter the most. That requires making decisions constantly, choosing what not to focus on or care about at that particular moment in time. Eighty percent of your outcome in your life results from 20 percent of all your causes or inputs for any given event.

OK, so how do you apply the Pareto Principle in your life or business? The principle is a concept that suggests two out of ten items; anything on any general to-do list will turn out worth more than the other eight items put together. The sad part is that most people will procrastinate on the top 10 or 20 percent of the items that are the most valuable and important and busy themselves instead with the least important 80 percent, the trivial items that contribute very little to their success.

A friend of mine in the retail business explained to me how he applied the 80/20 rule to achieve his goal of doubling his sales over the next three years. He applied the 80/20 rule to his client base. What he found was that 20 percent of his clients contributed 80 percent of his profits. He also found that the amount of time spent on a high-profit client was the same time on a low-profit client.

In other words, he was dividing his time equally over the number of tasks that he does, while only 20 percent of those items contributed to 80 percent of his results. So, he drew a line on his list of clients under those who represented the top 20 percent and then called in other professionals in his industry and very carefully, politely, and strategically handed off the 80 percent of his clients that only represented 20 percent of his business.

He then put together a profile of his top clients and began looking in the marketplace exclusively for the type of client who fit the profile, in other words, for one who could become a major profit contributor to his organization and whom he, in turn, could serve with the level of excellence that his clients were accustomed to. And instead of doubling his income in three to five years, he doubled it in the first year with that one simple time management technique!

The overwhelming reality is: we live in a world where almost everything is worthless, and very few things are exceptionally valuable. Less is always more. It's more than a time-management strategy or a productivity technique. It's a systematic discipline for finding what is absolutely essential, then eliminating everything that is not, so we can make the highest contribution toward the things that really matter.

Chapter 11

Life on autopilot

On April 13, 2011, I flew to China with a good friend. We flew first class with Delta Airlines. We had a chance to speak to the pilot, and he invited us to his cabin before the plane took off, showed us around, and how he flies the plane. He told us that the aircraft had four engines, but it only needed one. If any engine has a problem, the next engine picks up without noticing. He said we had a 12-hour flight to Tokyo. During that time, the plane will be on autopilot most of the time if there is no turbulence or bad weather.

The hardest part of flying a plane is the takeoff and landing. Once the plane reaches a certain altitude, it pretty much flies itself. It's similar to how the human mind functions; we are always on autopilot. Driving to work or home, all those mundane tasks you do during the day become automatic; there is nothing to think about doing exactly what we did yesterday by default. The mind rarely gets involved because it's already programmed for specific tasks. There is a bunch of tasks your brain kicks in on autopilot mode where some thinking or decision is supposed to be made.

Imagine you just drove home from work. You step out of your car, and I ask you how the trip was. You probably won't remember how often you switched lanes or stopped at a traffic light. But you got home safely, regardless. When you live on autopilot, it feels like someone else is driving, not you.

Our brains have developed an unconscious decision-making system so we can take care of routine tasks. It prevents us from overloading. However, modern life has hijacked our lives – the mechanism that is supposed to protect us is disengaging us from living.

Humans rarely live in the present. We wander between the past and the future all day long. I did that for years and still do. I exercise a lot and run a lot to practice being present and being here and now. Living on autopilot disengages us from both our present and our future.

We, humans, are creatures of habits and routines, which is not a bad thing. It serves us well at times. Science says that we make about 40,000 decisions every day. Our brains can't possibly take the time to consider every single thing we do. Imagine having to remember to get dressed or brush your teeth every day. Talk about decision overload. Whenever it can, your brain will kick into an automatic decision-making gear to save energy, freeing up your conscious mind to work on other mentally taxing things.

Your ability to unconsciously process tons of information and make decisions on autopilot at any given moment is a cognitive achievement that makes life easier. However, when this automatic feature starts slipping into other areas of your life that need more forethought, it comes at an emotional cost, your happiness.

"Autopilot has gone from being an evolutionary protection mechanism that stopped our brains from overloading to our default mode of operating whereby we sleepwalk into our choices," wrote Dr. Mark Williamson, the director of Action for Happiness. Professor Renata Salecl, a sociologist and philosopher, surveyed 3,000 people, of which 96 percent admitted to living on autopilot.

Another study by two Harvard University psychologists, Matthew Killingsworth and Daniel Gilbert, author of Stumbling on Happiness, revealed that the average person spends about half (47 percent) of their waking hours doing what they call "mind wandering."

Living on autopilot can leave you sleepwalking through life's pivotal moments, making it very difficult to make intentional decisions about how you want to work and live your life. Instead of making conscious choices about the food you eat, the clothes you wear, the people you spend time with, the things you buy, and the places you go, you make decisions by default. Over time these small mindless decisions can prevent you from reaching your full potential or your definition of success. Before you know it, you are living your life by default, not by design; you're wearing clothes you don't want to wear, you're driving a car you don't want to drive, or you are in a relationship you don't want to be in.

Here are ten signs you're living your life on autopilot:

-You dread the day ahead. You wake up and dread the day because there's nothing you're looking forward to. You don't feel excited or inspired to start the day because you have a pretty good idea of how unpleasant it will be.

-Your daily routine is predictable. You could practically tell someone how you'll spend your entire day a month from now. For example, you could tell them exactly where you'll go, what you'll do, who you'll see, and what you'll eat.

-You do things without thinking. You act without stopping to think about what you're doing, how you're doing it, and why you're doing it. Your decisions and actions have become so automatic that it takes little thought.

-You can't seem to put your phone down. You automatically check your phone for updates and mindlessly scroll through your emails or social media feed at every opportunity you get − even though you just checked it!

-You stay deep in thought. You constantly catch yourself deep in thoughts unrelated to what you're doing. You are thinking of something totally different. Basically, you're mentally checked out in "la la land."

-You have a difficult time remembering things. You're not fully present and don't remember doing activities like driving, eating, or having that conversation you should have remembered. You say you easily forget the "little things" and sometimes feel mentally mushy.

-You can't seem to let go. You do what's familiar even though you know it's not serving you well anymore. For example, you keep the same unmotivated and unambitious people around, stay in the same career, hold onto things you've outgrown, live in the same old place, and do things that don't inspire you because you're used to it.

-You're not making meaningful progress. You make little to no significant progress toward your goals as days, weeks, and months fly by. You're not focused on what's most important to you and feel down because of it.

-You say "yes" more than you say "no." You often agree to things you don't want to do, then dread the decision afterward. Instead of carefully considering your options, you've made "yes" your default answer. For example, you say "yes" to working late, hosting the family gathering, watching the kids, or going to a party when you'd rather stay home.

-You know there's a better life to be lived. You believe your life could be more joyous, but you feel stuck in your current situation. Deep down, you've settled into too many areas of your life and wish you would've taken a different path.

If one or more of these signs resonates with you, there's a high probability you're living your life on autopilot. I find myself thinking way too much. My wife usually catches me by saying, "There you go again with your thinking brain. What are you thinking now? Stop thinking! Get up and do something, like take the garbage out." I usually answer with a lie, "No, I was working on a problem in my head," but she knows I'm lying. Sometimes I'm on my phone too much, checking my emails like crazy. I'm not expecting emails from anyone, but I constantly check it even though I just checked it a minute ago. It's insane.

The good thing is that you can get your brain off autopilot and train it to wander less. This ability will result in conscious decision-making. You must act if you want to turn off the cruise control and create a more joyful and fulfilling life now. Rewire the brain and do things differently.

The first thing you can do is create a life vision. You must know where you are going and what you want to do with your precious life. You better be clear about what it is that you call a beautiful life for YOURSELF – not your mom, dad, husband, or wife. Once you know what you want, you can align your thoughts and actions.

Next, you can practice living in the moment and being mindful. Meditation helps me a lot. As soon as I wake up, I do my morning prayers and meditate for 15 to 20 minutes. I calm myself down, focus on my priorities, visualize my day from beginning to end – how I want it to unfold, expect the best to happen, and say to myself, "Today is a great day!" You always get what you expect in life.

Research has shown that we are happiest when our thoughts and actions are aligned. How you spend your day doesn't tell you much about how happy you are. Instead, your mental presence is a much better predictor of your happiness. So, the next time you're out in traffic, walking or jogging, or talking to someone, try to take note of what you see and how you feel in the moment. It's simple yet powerful. Being present will help you be more intentional in all areas of your life, allowing you to live by design, not by default.

When you are about to start doing something, pause to notice what you're doing. Set an intention to be fully devoted, single-mindedly devoted to this one thing. Then give it your everything, as if it were your last act.

Dandapani is a Hindu priest, entrepreneur, and a former monk of ten years. His mission is to help people live a purposeful life and spread joy by empowering them with tools and teachings used by Hindu monks of his tradition for thousands of years. He was asked one day how to develop mindfulness and self-discipline. He mentioned three things:

1. Finish what you begin.
2. Do more than you think you can.
3. Do a little better than you think you can.

All these things require effort to develop willpower. It's easier to start a project than to finish it. Halfway through a project, most people say to themselves, "Whose idea was this? It's too hard. I want to start something new!" To finish what you begin every time requires willpower. The practical way to bring this to your life is to look at your average day and ask yourself, "What are the mundane and repetitive things that I do every day?" Or you can ask this question, "What are the non-negotiable, reoccurring events in my life?"

For instance, you must sleep every day – that's a non-negotiable task. So, as most people do, you brush your teeth, put on your pajamas, go to bed, sleep for 6 to 8 hours, wake up, make the bed, and the process of sleep is finished. When I come home from work, I try not to go straight to relax or take a nap or watch TV with my work clothes on. I put away my keys, phone, shoes, and bag, shower, and change my clothes, and that ends the workday for me; now, I can take on another task. It helps me to be mindful to be present. Going to work is something we do every day. I try to be mindful of the process, and when I'm working, I try to stay focused on what I'm doing most of the time. Distraction gets in the way for sure, like my phone, social media, and so on, but I have to be mindful.

Living on autopilot means leaning towards the most comfortable thinking mode. But we have two thinking modes and must learn to use both. Nobel Prize-winning Professor Daniel Kahneman's book Thinking, Fast and Slow turned them mainstream.

"Mode 1" is an automatic, fast, and unconscious way of thinking – it's our autopilot. This system is autonomous and efficient, though deceiving, too. It's more prone to bias and repetitive errors.

"Mode 2" is slow, conscious, and effortful, requiring attention and energy. It's more reliable and can filter out the misjudgments of Mode 1.

The brain is lazy. That's why it leans towards Mode 1. You got to be aware and train your mind to avoid being on autopilot. One mode is not better than the other, but the secret lies in using both in a balanced way.

"Mode 1" is ideal for quick decisions based on little information. When you are driving your car or doing the laundry, you don't need to overthink. However, you wouldn't use it to make more significant life choices, like your career, which homes to buy, or whom to marry.

"Mode 2" is ideal for handling more complex mental activities, such as logical reasoning, managing interpersonal relationships, learning new things, and building habits. It can help you turn off the autopilot.

The 1952 Nobel peace prize winner, Dr. Albert Schweitzer, said that the problem with people today is that they don't think and use only 10% of their brain capacity.

Awareness is also vital. That's how you know where your mind is at any given time. You will need to practice extended daily meditation to get to the point where you find yourself constantly in the present moment. Humans rarely operate in the present, and the present is where you can build your future. So, how can you improve yourself when you are rarely in the present?

Brain researchers said 90% of your decisions on a day-to-day basis are automated from your subconscious by the time you turn 30. Once you get past that growth or development stage majority of us are on autopilot.

Find a different route going or coming from work so you can pay attention. You tend to pay attention more when it's new than when it's old and familiar. It's like a new relationship in that you want to invest time to get to know the person better, to jell together, to surprise the person. When you're dating for the first time or in love, you tend to be there and present all the time compared to when you have been married for ten years. You know your partner very well. Your mind has it figured out already, so you tend to take each other for granted because there is nothing more to discover. That's why it's essential to do things differently in your marriage, change it up, spice things up, don't be so predictable, and challenge yourselves to new stuff. Be spontaneous, find new hobbies, compete for the world's best speaker or something. If you go left all the time, go right today, disrupt your routine, make new friends, learn a new language, put your watch on your right wrist instead of the left one, change your normal, and rearrange your rooms. All changes require new thinking.

Stop doing the daily task that doesn't count, and question everything. Time management is self-management. There is no such thing as managing time because you can't save, store, or stop it. Time will keep going regardless of what you do, and you only can manage yourself by knowing how you spend that time. That's why starting the day with a good plan, knowing your outcome for today, is good.

Refrain from throwing yourself aimlessly at the day with no action plan, about to repeat the previous unproductive day. At the end of every day, you should seriously sit down, get your journal, and review day. Ask yourself how it was today and what did I accomplish today. That's how you measure your progress and what gets measured gets improved1.

Chapter 12

Fear of failure

"When it feels scary to jump that is exactly when you jump, otherwise you end up staying in the same place your whole life, and that I can't do".

In 1901, Theodore Roosevelt considered inviting Booker T. Washington to the White House for dinner. It would be the first time in American history that a black man had dined as a sitting president's guest.

But Roosevelt hesitated. He was scared of what his Southern relatives might think—what the newspapers would say. Scared that racist voters would abandon him, that he would lose support in the South, and that it could cost him the election.

News of the dinner between a former slave and the president of the United States became a national sensation. The subject of inflammatory articles and cartoons shifted the national conversation around race at the time.

"African-Americans were invited to meet in offices. They built the White House. They worked for various presidents. But they were never invited to sit at the president's table. And when that happened, the outrage was just unbelievable.

'Dining,' and I put it in quotation marks, was a code word for social equality. And the feeling was, certainly in the South, that if you invited a man to sit at your table, you were inviting him to woo your daughter. He should feel perfectly comfortable asking your daughter to marry him. And so that's the primary reason why people were so offended. It just shouldn't happen in 1901 when segregation was law.

"Theodore Roosevelt was known for being a very impulsive man. But this was a good impulse. "The very fact that I felt a moment's qualm on inviting him because of his color made me ashamed of myself," Roosevelt said in a letter, "and made me hasten to send the invitation.

"Now, Booker T. Washington faced the same thing when he had to decide whether or not to accept the invitation. He thought, 'This will be a real problem for me, but I have no right to refuse. It's a landmark moment, and I must accept this on behalf of my whole race.'...

As things turned out, I am delighted that I asked him, for the clamor aroused by the act makes me feel as if the action was necessary." Said the President

But in the end, it was precise because he was scared that he did it.

There are more things likely to frighten us than there are to crush us.

I define fear as some abstract hole in the ground that you dig for yourself, and you are the only one who knows it's there. Fear will make you dig your grave and put you in there if you are not careful. There is no such thing as being fearless, everyone feels some fear in their lives, but the difference is in how they handle those fears. Do you let it stop you, make you give up? Or do you "Feel The Fear and Do It Anyway" regardless of how you feel about it? I will instead do the latter because there's no gain if there's no pressure.

Ryan Holiday, author of "Courage is calling," said

do the thing you are scared to do. Because where we experience resistance, hesitation, reluctance is often evidence of progress or the potential for it.

The cage you're scared to enter holds the treasure you are looking for. Be aware of your feelings and how you feel about doing certain things. Make sure you realize that you must face your fears to grow. Doing it now is the best way to get it done because if you know that you have to pass this way to get to your destination, waiting or procrastinating before you do the work will make the task even more daunting and harder to achieve. Use the fear to direct you. Most likely, what you fear doing is the exact thing you need to do now.

When Coach Bob suggested that I sign up at Toastmasters to improve my communication skills, I was scared; I did not want to go, I was trying to find my way around that, but he insisted that I should go.

Toastmasters is a non-profit educational program to help you speak in public, and there is a club in almost every town in the US and overseas. Being a scary cat, there was no way I would stand in front of people to say anything, but I took my courage with two hands and went for it. My first days were brutal.

After the meeting, I decided not to go back the following week. This is not me. I can't do this public speaking stuff. It won't work for me." I needed to Face my fear. I needed to Understand it and Control it. So he forced me to sign up to become a member.

The club told me that I had to give ten speeches, each from five to seven minutes in length, and they would evaluate every speech to provide me with feedback. I received a manual with all the guidelines that I needed to follow. I said to myself, "Ten speeches!!! What??? You have to be kidding!" My first speech was due in 2 weeks. During those two weeks, all I was thinking about was the speech. I was so anxious, nervous, and fearful the whole time. "What am I going to talk about?" I was still determining what the topic of my speech would be. I wanted to call them and reschedule, cancel, and be excused. I was scared because I did not know what to talk about and how to do it. People who do public speaking are not ordinary. They're different. He insisted on not rescheduling or canceling the speech; he said, "When you put yourself on the line where there is no turning back, your mind will find a way for you." That's precisely what happened. Someone said, "You don't know how strong you are until being strong is your only option." The first speech was an ice-breaking speech in which I mainly talked about myself. The first and second speeches were a disaster, but facing my fears gave me ideas for combating them. I started to get involved in reading about my topic and the things I wanted to discuss. I read many nonfiction books and watched videos on YouTube to understand and control my fear.

By the time I reached my tenth speech, I was the best speaker in the club and competed for the World's Best Speaker, representing my club. I was alive for the first time in my life. I became comfortable on the stage, and I was free. I did something that I thought was impossible. It would not scare me anymore. I was not hiding anymore. I was ready to stand on podiums. I started to dream about being a public speaker. I began to follow Tony Robbins, Les Brown, and Zig Ziglar. I visited Canada to see Tony, Les, and other speakers first-hand. When you decide to face your fear, opportunities start to open for you. You begin to grow.

The number one fear is the fear of failure. Nobody wants to fail, and I get that. But fear of failure is a significant obstacle between you and your goals. To deal with this type of fear, you need to be clear about what you consider failure—giving up—never going after your dreams—not achieving your desired outcome within an expected timeline? What is your definition of failure? Be clear about the obstacles on your way to your goals.

Inside every human being is a desire to pursue wild ambitions and discover new possibilities. There's a would-be entrepreneur, motivational speaker, freelance writer, stage performer, or off-the-grid traveler in all of us. But unfortunately, most people spend their lives in a routine, nondescript comfort zone because they're too intimidated to chase a goal that seems uncertain and prone to fail. According to a 2016 survey, 34.2 million Americans experience some phobia. The most common is a fear of personal failure, which most define as unemployment, financial ruin, and isolation from others. To make your goal pursuit fail-proof, switch from thinking about failures to thinking about discrepancies between what you hope to achieve and what you might achieve. Discrepancies provide information you can study, explain, and learn to recalibrate your future efforts. As long as you continue making an effort, there is no room for failure. When you give up altogether, for no better reason than fear of failing, that's a different story!

Fear is our response to two kinds of threats: real and imagined. It would help if you distinguished between these threats. You already know the difference. Real threats pose a risk to our survival. Imagined threats are hypothetical scenarios. Delivering a speech in front of a group of people is an imagined threat because there is little risk to your survival. Delivering a speech in front of a pride of lions in the savanna is a real threat because they are not interested in hearing you. They are more interested in eating you. By definition, fear of failure involves imagined threats. And while the fear is accurate, the threat is not. For the time being, the threat is a prediction, a product of your imagination, a scenario you built. This doesn't make your fear unfounded or irrational. But it makes it premature and unnecessary. Instead of letting it stop you, study it and plan to avoid the consequences you're scared of.

Fear of failure is the intense worry you experience when you imagine all the horrible things that could happen if you fail to achieve a goal. Extreme anxiety increases the odds of holding back or giving up. Being successful relies, to a large extent, on your ability to leverage fear. Fear will create hesitation, and hesitation will develop doubts. If you fixate on doubts too long, it will create anxiety, and then you lose that window of opportunity – it's gone.

We need to own and control things that are the root of all fears. We hold on to ideas we have about ourselves, to the material possessions and standard of living that we think to define us. That is the monkey mind thinking. The monkey is always thinking about what it's getting. I read the book Think Like a Monk by Jay Shetty. He said that a Monk practice detachment, not attachment. The actual cause of fear is attachment, and the cure is detachment. Clinging to temporary things gives them power over us, and they become a source of pain and anxiety. We own nothing; everything is borrowed. When you die, you will take nothing with you. Treat everything you own as things you borrowed, enjoy, have fun with, and stop overprotecting or fear of losing it. Act like you're the guy who rented a luxury car; you won't tell yourself that you own it if you rented the car for a week in some way that allows you to enjoy it even more. You borrowed it, and you're grateful for the chance to drive it around town.

Imagine you rented a luxury five stars hotel in downtown Manhattan, with a jacuzzi, hot tub, chef kitchen, and ocean views: beautiful and exciting. I bet you won't spend any time dreading your departure in a week. When we acknowledge that all our blessings are like a fancy five stars hotel or luxury car, we are free to enjoy them without fear of losing them. We are all lucky vacationers enjoying our stay in Hotel Earth. Detachment is the ultimate practice of minimizing fear.

In Senegal or any other Muslim country, the biggest fear for most women is not getting married, and that's an attachment. That's how they define their life. They have to be married for their lives to be meaningful. Some wind up marrying the wrong guy to get the status of married. Instead, they should practice detachment from that belief. Not requiring the husband in the first place is how they will get the husband. Not needing anything attracts everything.

I got this expression "FU*K FEAR" from self-defense expert Tony Blauer. He said that "Fu*k Fear" is a process for managing fear. The F stands for Face your fear. When you commit to facing it, you then move to Understand it. Next, you research it by Googling it, reading a book about it, or hiring a coach or mentor to help you understand it better. These things do not eliminate fear but can dissolve their hold on you. So, it moves from an emotional place to a place where you can Control and Confront it. That is where the K comes in. K is to Know it and put it in perspective. It's vital to understand that fear does not dissipate. You don't eradicate fear. Everybody wants to be where there is no fear, but it does not exist. There will always be a stimulus, a new concern that will trigger some physiological response, and you will get into that same cycle again. However, if you understand, control, and know your fear, it will not stop you from moving forward.

Fear stands for False Evidence, Appearing Real. It's not real; it only exists in your head. When you try to do something that you fear, don't get in your head; if you do, trust me, you will be negotiating with yourself – should I do it, or should I wait, or I might not make it, I might fail, it's risky – fear kicks in and you're dead. It gets in your way when you overthink or wait too long. It will paralyze or cripple you in some way to stop you from moving.

You are strong, and you can prevail. Fear of failure is not about the challenges ahead or the effort required. It is about the consequences we may suffer if we fail. We are not afraid of the work we have to do but of the remote chance that our work will not be good enough to yield results that meet our standards. Researchers on fear of failure have identified several negative consequences people with a fear of failure expect, including feelings of shame and embarrassment, a big blow to self-esteem, the prospect of an uncertain future, and the loss of social influence. Notice that people estimate the psychological cost of failing to be much higher than the material cost. People who fear failure are less worried about losing money than about losing friends, Faces, or faith. To further reduce your fear of failure, identify the consequences of failing that scare you the most and evaluate your ability to deal with these consequences. Instead of talking yourself out of fear by hoping that nothing adverse will happen, focus on building confidence to deal with the results.

Here are some questions to ask yourself:

Which of the consequences scares you the most?

How much impact will they have on you?

Are they merely unpleasant, or are they life-threatening?

Will they make you uncomfortable or hurt you deeply and irreparably?

How quickly will you move on?

Are the consequences permanent or reversible?

Are they short-lived, or will they linger forever?

How well can you handle them?

Can you exercise damage control, or will you hide and disappear?

Les Brown said when you become fearless, life becomes limitless. I agree. A few years ago, I had to deliver a speech in front of an audience to be selected for the World's Best Speaker contest. After the speech, I was so in love with myself. I told myself the sky was the limit. It boosted my self-confidence from ten to a thousand. I started to value myself more because I felt like I did something that most people can't imagine doing since most fear public speaking. When you face the things that you fear, it runs away.

In her book Feel the Fear and Do It Anyway, Susan Jeffers said, "If everyone feels fear when approaching something new in life, yet so many are out there doing it despite the fear, then we must conclude that fear is not the problem. You are innately designed to use your power. When you don't, you experience helplessness, paralysis, and depression."

Here are seven quotes that I got from Susan's book that I want to share with you to end this chapter:

"Taking responsibility means being aware of where and when you are not taking responsibility so that you can eventually change."

"See if you can go one week without criticizing anyone or complaining about anything."

"No one is immune to pain, and it shouldn't be denied when it exists. The key is knowing that you can lead a productive and meaningful life no matter the external circumstances. Positive thinking offers a power boost to help you handle whatever life gives."

"Most of us are not aware that we belong to the moan-and-groan crowd until we stop moaning and groaning . . . Among the new friends you make, including those who are farther along the journey than you are."

"We have been taught to believe that negative equals realistic, and positive equals unrealistic."

"If all your giving is about getting, think how fearful you will become."

"Whatever it takes, feel the fear, press on, and do it anyway!"

One of Seneca's most famous quotes is, "we suffer more imagination than in reality." What he's trying to say is you don't have to suffer in advance. Anxiety is a punishment to yourself; it doesn't resolve the situation. It just makes you nervous, uncomfortable, and miserable. It often brings about exactly what you fear in the first place, so be prepared for what life can throw at you, but you don't suffer before you

need to because you know that it doesn't do anything about
the situation.

Chapter 13

Jockey and Horse race

"There is no passion to be found playing small in settling for a life that is less than the one you're capable of living. Nelson Mandela

I worked for NCR from 2008-2018. In 2008 we met the CEO, Bill Nuti; he came to the Long Island office and wanted to talk to us about the company's future. He spoke about how the company was doing financially despite the recession in 2008, the layoffs, and cutdowns. An employee of 30 years got up and asked Bill how come they were getting a 20% pay cut after all these years of hard work they endured working for NCR. Bill apologized and said he did not know about it. However, at the end of the same year, he collected 11 million dollars in bonuses. This is the definition of a horse and Jockey race. The jockey always gets the prize while the horse(employee) is constantly being trained and beaten up to run better and faster.

Merriam-Webster dictionary needs to add two new words in their books. Youtuber and Tik Toker. Do you know Youtubers make 6 or 7 figures incomes quickly just by talking about what they're passionate about? You are talking about yourself, what you like, and getting paid. I see a youtube channel with millions of views talking about nothing and getting paid. Youtube loves content; they will rank your video higher if it's good to keep people on the platform. Some people say technology is killing the job market. It thinks it made it easier to make money. How many people are living off the Taxi Ride App Uber? It creates millions of jobs; opportunities are all over the world.

You create content on YouTube, and you get a check. YouTube will train you to do just that. You can also use other people's content and still make money. Instead of going to the bank to open an IRA account for your retirement, go on youtube.com and learn how to create content. Thousands of other YouTubers will help you. Find topics you like to discuss and let the AI generate the content. Affiliate marketing with Amazon or other e-commerce retail shops will also pay you. You drive traffic to their site from youtube by making an explainer video on how to use a product and using the affiliate marketing link in the description to drive people to buy, and you get a check. You do that religiously for six months. You won't need a job.

Go on Google and type chatGPT; this artificial intelligence created by Open Ai will do the work for you. It will write python code for you, write you a book, and even make youtube videos for you. You don't have to say a word or show your face. The robot does all the work for you. Teachers are going nuts because students are using it to do their homework.

Now is the best time ever to be human. This is the easiest time to make millions using a little bit of creativity. You can start a business with no money and make millions. In this age of social media, YouTube, Tik Tok, NFTs, Instagram, Facebook, and so on, you can pick one of these platforms, master it in a few months and start earning money by sharing what you know.

The most viewed children's music video on YouTube, and the most viewed video overall, is "Baby Shark" by Pinkfong (Republic of Korea), with over 10 billion views as of December 22nd, 2022. First uploaded on June 18th, 2016, the catchy singalong is sung by Hope Segoine, a Korean-American girl who was ten years old. According to a BBC report, the creators of Baby Shark earned $283,000 a month from YouTube streams alone.

This kid video earned millions of dollars on YouTube, and the video is only 2 min long. This is crazy. There is so much stupid stuff to do to make money on this platform, where people are begging for your content. Is it necessary to get an MBA, Accounting degree, or 100K student loan and hope to get a job to pay for the loan?

Comedian Khaby Lame has become the king of Tik-

Tok -- all without uttering a word. With more than 142.9 million followers, Lame has dethroned teen dancer and content creator Charli D'Amelio to become the most-followed person on the platform.

Lame, 22, born in the West African nation of Senegal and now lives in Italy, creates videos in which he reacts wordlessly to absurd life hacks, racking up millions of views and likes with each post. I see Lame in the media with Mark Zuckerburg and Snoop Dogg with other legends in the business. Lame still did not say a word in his videos. We're living in the most exciting time, we're all on these social media platforms, and we're closer than ever before. It does not matter where you are; you can make millions by leveraging technology. If you are broke right now, it's on you. You're the problem, not the country you're living in, your government, not your mom or dad. Stop overthinking, and make your moves like Khaby lame. I do know another Senegalese kid in Senegal, this guy lives at the far end in a remote village, and he made so much noise that the whole country took notice. I watched his videos he's saying nothing beneficial. Now TV is interviewing him, and businesses are contacting him. It's mindblowing what technology can do for you. Turn your device into a money-making machine.

I bought my niece Sophic an Ipad, and she made a one-minute video on Tick Tock unpacking the Ipad and turning it on for the first time. By the time she woke up, more than a thousand people had seen it. It's easy to get exposure for your business, whatever you're selling. Distribution on these social media platforms is free. YouTube is where you can learn anything. Nowadays, any information you need about any subject is on the internet. College courses are offered online thru Coursera. You download the app and can go to college for $39.99 a month. MBA courses are offered on Coursera for a meager price compared to 10 years ago. The information you need to do whatever you want with your life is already in your pocket. All you need to do is pull out your device and apply it yourself.

You can sell anything on Amazon in the USA and internationally and earn millions. You can set up shop online with Shopify, sell anything and get products in front of your customers overnight. If you need to learn how to market your product, you can hire someone on Fiverr.com or Upwork.com to do it for you for a meager price. Millions of freelancers worldwide offer their services almost free on these sites I just mentioned. You can have virtual employees worldwide doing great work for you. I hired a bunch of them in the past years.

Chefs or cooks out there, find a local restaurant, rent space in their kitchen, cook your food, and list it on Uber Eats, Door Dash, or Grubhub, and cash in. You don't need to open a restaurant, rent space in a kitchen, and sell your food online. There is a company in the US that help you do just that. The possibilities to make money are endless. You're on the wrong path when you see yourself working too hard for your little money, said Author and motivational speaker Jack Canfield. "Change your mind about money, it's not hard to make, but you have to be willing to learn." Go on YouTube now and type how to make money, millions of videos on that subject. You can't be ignorant these days; Ignorance equals poverty and Pain. Be willing to stretch yourself just a little bit, learn, and participate in your own rescue.

Stop looking for employment and look for deployment. To be employed means somebody benefits from your energy; to deploy yourself means using your power to be productive. Instead of waiting for someone to give you a job or to get a better job, create your own work. Your job is what you've been trained to do, and your work is what you were born to do. Your job is your skills, and your employer can fire you anytime. Your work is your gift, and no one can take that from you. Your job is where you get compensation for activity, and your work is where you get fulfillment because you love it so much. You can retire from your job, not your work, because your work is you. When the person discovers their work, they no longer need a job.

Every problem in life is a business opportunity. All businesses are simply someone solving a problem. There are so many business opportunities in these third countries, and very often in Senegal, friends of mine and people complain about a bunch of things going wrong in the country. I al-

ways tell them to stop looking at it as a problem, look at it as
business opportunity and start thinking about how you can
solve this issue. The problem you face is not just yours alone;
many people have the same problem. Find ways to solve that
problem. The more problem you solve, the more money you
have. We need this mindset. We're trained to get a job rather
than to start a business. We're taught to be employed, not
prepared to deploy ourselves.

Thank God today is Friday; why? or Happy Friday!
I have never heard happy Monday. Were you in Jail from
Monday – Thursday? Studies say that 71% of Americans
work at a job they don't like until they retire. I think it's sad
that some people are thrilled on Fridays. Work takes most of
your time. Wouldn't you want to do something you love so
that every day feels like Friday? You can't put off happiness
until you retire one day. Some people will never believe they
can be their own boss, retire young and be financially free.
You're in charge of your happiness. You must be happy now,
no matter what; you're in charge of that.

Don't blame the boss; blame yourself. Find a side hustle
and get started. You can find something else. The world is
full of choices and possibilities to make money regardless of
where you are, and if you're in the USA, that's even better.
In social media, opportunities are endless to earn a living.
Everybody got a voice, and your voice can be heard. I know
a guy who buys stuff at a garage sale or thrift store and sells
them on eBay, making $5000 a month for just 2 to 3 hours

of work daily.

You get trapped in the financial matrix; you work for somebody and never break free. It would help if you found a way to create excess cash and make investments that work for you while you sleep, Robinhood is here, and countless other apps to help you. You need to put your ass on a chair, sit there, focus without being disturbed, and read. If you don't have any money, use sweat equity by going to work for somebody and then use your time and equity to make them money. You can't start at the top. You start out at the bottom.

Operate from the standpoint of duty and logic. You just can't wing it. People say, "I'm just going to freewheel today." You can either act from an animal side, which is to wing it through life, or operate from a sense of logic and duty. Learn and hang out with people who aren't beholding to the man. Find people with discipline who are self-motivated from within, and spend time with them.

I worked at Amazon, doing deliveries for them. It was the worst job of my life. The company is customer-driven, and they don't give a damn about their employees. Amazon will suck the blood out of you. I was one of the best drivers they had. I was on point, never late, never wasted company time, and was honest with them. Some of my coworkers used to say that I loved the job. It was about doing the right thing by them. You don't have to like your job to do the right thing. After my shifts with Amazon, I would check myself in the library to work on myself, reading, writing this book, planning, and studying my next move.

Don't be a horse all your life – break out, call your shots, level up. Try to be a jockey at least once, and free yourself of the rat race. Create your world, and go for financial freedom. Live your life on your terms. It's mind-blowing how many fun things to do in this world.

In my first years in America, I lived in Delaware with my brother. Having access to learning tools for free was amazing and mind-blowing to me. Some people might think I am exaggerating, but I'm not. It's standard here in the USA that every town has its library. It's not the case in some other countries. That's why I urge my American friends to travel out of the country, so they can appreciate the opportunities they have in America.

I am sold on reading. I get up at 5:00 am to read. I have collected over a thousand books in counting. I am learning from Business strategist Tony Robbins, billionaire investor Warren Buffett, and Netflix co-founder Marc Randolph. Those books helped me a lot growing up. The Garden City Library by my house gives away hundreds of great books throughout the year. Books like the story of Nike – how Phil knight built his NIKE empire from $50 – and countless other great books were out there in front of the library for free, and very few people stopped to look.

You have to be more to earn more – it's that simple.

Don't complain about the raise or the promotion you're not getting. It's the value that you are bringing to the marketplace –. As Cal Newport puts it in his best-seller book, you must be so good at your craft that they can't ignore you. That's what is going to give you more money." For things to change, you have to change

I understand that all "jockeys" used to be great "horses ."You can start by being a horse but don't stay there. Break out of that and find your calling–that will make your life satisfying. Jockeys always find a way to make the horse run better, faster, and more productive, but at the end of the year, the jockey(boss) gets the bonus, while the horse (you) is left with the crumbs. Oh, you'll get an excellent review for being an outstanding employee with lousy raise that doesn't match your efforts.

One day I was off at Amazon, and I decided to spend all day at the library to work on this book. I'm a library junkie. My wife asked me, "Why are you working so hard? You don't take any days off for yourself." I told her that since I hate my job, I am doing whatever it takes to get the hell out, find something better, do something that I love, and I am the only one that can make that happen.

We know what to do but rarely do what we know. It's not about the strategy. The information to change whatever you want is free to grab. How bad do you want to change? Are you willing to do whatever it takes to change? Are you ready to get up at 5:00 am to work on yourself, instill self-disciplined routines, and work on winning habits to change your outcome?

Motivational speaker Jim Rohn said, "Work harder on yourself than you work on your job because if you work hard on your job, you will make a living, and if you work hard on yourself, you will make a fortune." He also said, "Income seldom exceeds personal development." We see it all the time when people who win the lotto become instant millionaires, but after a couple of years, they run out of money because of their poor mindset. You must cultivate a millionaire's mind to keep a million dollars, and that's hard work. The inner self has to be right first because you are just a reflection of your inner self.

Amazon has made many millionaires; 80 percent of the products sold on Amazon are from other people and companies worldwide. Their platform helps people like me to sell overseas in India, France, Japan, and so on, and anyone can get a piece of that pie. And you can log on to Fiverr.com to find freelancers who can help you sell on Amazon. You can find products to sell and suppliers to buy from. You can build your website or app, and so on. Facebook, Instagram, and TikTok can help you market your product; anyone can dominate.

It's a flat world we're living in now; leverage it. You can hire employees for $3 per hour on Fiverr or Upwork. I found an architect from India who works for $10 an hour. You can find web developers, app developers, and people who can help you live your dreams in China, and it's cheap. I have people in other countries begging for work, designers who can do mind-blowing work for almost nothing.

Tim Ferris has a great book, "4hr workweek". He teaches you how you can have people around the world doing your work for cheap while you somewhere in Gran Canyon sipping on some pina Colada and counting the stars.

There are 365 days in a year. How can you let someone or a company tells you how many days you can go on vacation? It's all about living life on my terms as soon as possible, not when I retire, old and frail; that's how I define success. You have the tools at your disposal to be a jockey – use them, and create a new world for yourself. Retool yourself, learn, and invest in educating yourself because Ignorance equals poverty and pain.

Chapter 14

We procastinate

"Procastination is the thief of time"
Charles Dickens

Tony was a popular butcher in Poland. People love to buy meat from him. Everything is fresh and at a reasonable price. He provides excellent customer service. His store stays crowded throughout the year. He has a tricky sign by his register: "Today you pay, tomorrow it's free." New customers always look at the sign puzzled. What does it mean? Does it mean I have to pay Today and tomorrow I won't?

Some customers took him up on that offer and returned the next day. They showed the receipt that they were here the day before. But the butcher showed them the sign and said, "Today you pay; tomorrow is free. So, you have to pay today again." He meant that the tomorrow you're looking for will never come; it will always be Today. Stop putting off things until tomorrow and do them now. If you don't feel like it Today, you likely won't feel like doing it tomorrow, either.

If you always postpone things until tomorrow, you will never do them. For example, expecting to start the business, speaking to your boss about a raise, going to the gym, or doing whatever the next day, you are delaying things until the tomorrow that will never come. You got to get on it and do it now. You can only build on what you are doing, not what you will do. Just do it, like the Nike slogan. Now really matters, and that's all we have.

Avoiding doing a task that needs to be accomplished by a specific deadline could be further stated as a habitual or intentional delay in starting or finishing a job despite knowing it might have negative consequences – that's the definition of procrastination.

My wife said that I am ridiculously good at procrastination -She tells me that all the time. I love to put stuff off until later, even when I know I can do them now. But sometimes, I don't see that as procrastination. It's just an intentional delay; no need to do it now; it can wait.

I do not want to be busy doing everything, continuously putting out fires. I like to put things in perspective, such as tasks that have something to do with my goals. I always put my attention where it matters the most and does things that I love to do so. No one procrastinates on things that they love to do. If you get yourself involved in tasks that you are not in tune with you, you tend to push them to the side.

It takes efforts building muscle, or losing weight. It's a psychological behavior when people don't believe in themselves. Or they might think that they don't deserve a gorgeous body, it's not for them, it's too far to reach, or it's a lot of work. They think that losing weight is impossible and it's a lost fight. Sometimes people can be emotionally too weak to push themselves to achieve their desired results.

Your emotions get in the way all the time. You want to get up and go to the gym to work out, but your mind says, "Oh, I don't feel like getting up; I'm too tired; it's cold outside, let's wait; after work, I will feel much better." You must be emotionally intelligent to push yourself to do things you know you should and do them regardless of how you feel about them. The mind is the battleground. You have to win that battle first.

We live in a building where there is a gym, which is big enough and has nice equipment. My wife asked me to coach her to get in shape, and I said, Fine, I will be your trainer. Just after a few days, I noticed she started to lose motivation. I wanted to know why, so I asked, but she did not say. I found out that every day after a workout, she weights herself. She expected the weight to start dropping right away, instant gratification mindset. I took the scale away. I told her, "Forget the scale. Let's focus on building a habit of going to the gym daily – that's the goal. Let's start small, like 15 to 20 minutes a day. That should be good enough. When planning, makes sure you think big; when progressing, think small. Let's make it an easy task so that you won't procrastinate. You got to play a trick on your mind. Make the task so effortless that it will be easy to build that habit. After that, you can raise the intensity level just a little and then continue adding a little weekly until you reach the desired level. A slow and steady pace will win the race. Consistent is the name of the game. The goal is not to lose weight but to be healthy. Forget about the scale. Just stay committed – that's it. It's a marathon, not a damn sprint."

Willpower is a huge factor when it comes to fitness. I remember driving to the gym every day, rain or shine. But now it's super convenient since the gym is just a couple of flights down from our apartment. Having the gym right at home wouldn't make a difference if you don't have the willpower to use it. Just like you can lead a horse to water, but you can't make it drink. That's why willpower and determination are the real keys to success. Even if the gym is miles away, if you have those two things, you'll find a way to get there.

You don't have to be great to start, but you have to start to be great.   Zig Ziglar.

I have been putting off writing this book you're reading right now for about three years. I kept delaying, waiting for the "right time" to get inspired. The primary issue was not that I was procrastinating but the fear of failing, not being good, and worrying about what people would say if I failed to deliver and if the book turned out a flap. So what if it's a flap? Dust yourself up and try again, said Zig Ziglar, the master motivator. Caring about what other thinks will kill your growth; you will always be their prisoner. How you eat an elephant that's how you write a book. Get started one bite at a time, one page at a time.

Being focused and grounded will help you beat any procrastinating. We tend to give ourselves too many things to do. My "ToDo" list used to be significant. I put everything on it, but only a few of the tasks were getting done. I overloaded myself right at the start. Instead of putting the essential tasks first, those tasks that, once done, would make you feel fabulous. I put them last. I needed to gain some momentum before I got to them." I was dead wrong. I was constantly procrastinating, and when the time came to do them, I said to myself, "Let me take a break. I need to check eBay. I'll browse Google first." I had all kinds of excuses to avoid getting started, and nothing was getting done; I kept delaying.

Motivational speaker Brian Tracy said it best: "Eat the frog first. Start with the most challenging task first – that's your frog. Get that out of the way. Schedule five or ten minutes to start on it. That's how you gain good momentum, and everything will become easy.

Getting up at 5 am to work is my frog, the most challenging task of the day; if I manage to get that out of the way, I will be a winner that day.

It can be conducive to having an accountability buddy. One fun way to take this a step further is to have a bet with your buddy. Choose a day and time within the next week that you will complete a task and then tell your friend or colleague: "I'll give you $20 or take you out to lunch or buy you coffee or watch that awful movie you've been wanting to see, whatever if I haven't completed this task by next Wednesday at 10:00 am." Give your accountability buddy a date and time within the next week and tell him to redeem the agreed-upon prize; he must check in with you on that appointed day and time. If you still need to complete your task by then, you owe them whatever you bet!

Waiting is a trap. You're always going to find reasons to wait. Tomorrow is the day you think you will have time to do the work. You think that your schedule will be lighter tomorrow to get started to work on their goals, their most important priorities. People wait to "feel like it" – that's a trap. I was waiting to "feel like" writing this book, waiting to get started. That's why it took me way almost five years to finish.

Before Anthony Burgess became a famous author in the 40s, he was diagnosed with a brain tumor and informed by the doctors that he had only one year to live. At the time, Burgess was broke and thought he had nothing to leave behind for his wife, Lynne. Burgess always knew that he had a writing talent. He thought it would be a good idea to publish a novel to leave royalties behind for Lynne. One year should be enough, he thought. So, he put a piece of paper into a typewriter and began writing. Of course, he knew that the publishers would likely reject his novel, but he couldn't think of anything else to do at the time. "It was January of 1960," he said, "and according to the prognosis, I had a winter and spring and summer to live through and would die with the fall of the leaf." Burgess was focused and wrote energetically from early morning until late at night. Before the year was through, he finished five and a half novels.

Contrary to the doctors' predictions, his cancer went into remission, and when that year was over, Burgess did not die. The tumor disappeared altogether. Burgess, best known for A Clockwork Orange, began his long and successful career as a novelist. Over the years that followed, he wrote more than 70 novels. Without the death sentence for his disease, he may not have started writing at all. Like Anthony Burgess, many of us hide an extraordinary talent, but most of the time, we never start working on it. What would you do if you, like Burgess, had just a year to live? Would you live differently? Would you try to discover your full potential before it is too late?

Jim Rohn said there are only two pains in life – the pain of regret and the pain of discipline. Regret weighs a ton, but discipline weighs just ounces. We all have an expiration date, Some people think they have thousand years to live, and they're taking their sweet time on everything, going through life in slow motion. I'm telling you to pick up the pace, be in a hurry, Stop playing small, stop procrastinating, and stop waiting for the right time. Give up the drop and become the ocean. There are books in you, business ideas in you, and more life in you, but it can only be done through you. How you play that instrument, that song, that piano, can only be done by you. Some ideas are unique to you. You owe it to the world to bring forth your dreams and aspirations. No one else will do it for you.

Chapter 15

Winner's mindset

A long time ago, a great warrior was about to send his armies against a powerful foe whose men outnumbered his own. He knew he had to come up with a decision that would ensure his success on the battlefield. He loaded his soldiers into boats and sailed to the enemy's country. When the soldiers and equipment were unloaded, he gave the order to burn the ships that had carried them. Addressing his men before the first battle, he said, "You see the boats going up in smoke. That means that we cannot leave these shores alive unless we win! Now we have no choice – we win or perish!" They won. Every person who wins at any undertaking must be willing to burn his ship and cut all sources of retreat. Only by doing so can anyone be sure of maintaining that state of mind known as a burning desire to win.

The 1997 NBA Draft included Kobe Bryant, Marcus Camby, Allen Iverson, Ray Allen, Steve Nash, Jermaine O'Neal, Stephon Marbury, and Tracy McGrady. That 1997 Draft still has more Most Valuable Players than any other year. Fifty-seven players were chosen from 353 college basketball teams with a total number of roughly over 3500 players if you consider that each College team has only ten players. The competition to get into the NBA is fierce, so those 57 players fought hard to get into the NBA.

However, only 15% of this group was recognized as elite basketball players like Kobe, Iverson, Nash, and so on. What happened to the rest? Most of them had a mindset like "I will keep working hard until I get to the NBA." So, they were just satisfied to make the NBA league. In contrast, Kobe's mentality, for example, was, "I did not come this far only to come this far." Staying successful is the hardest. If you reach the top of the mountain, find a bigger one. It's always a journey. There is no destination. The continued pursuit of growth, the constant seeking of improvement, the challenge – those are the things that make life great. Be proud but never satisfied, proud but forever hungry.

A true winner seeks more than the title. A true winner seeks growth and greatness. In June 1992, 76ers Charles Barkley was traded to the Phoenix Suns, and the Sixers received three players – Jeff Hornacek, Tim Perry, and An-drew Lang. Can you believe Charles Barkley was worth those three players? I would have retired right there if I were one of those three players. Some players' goals were to get into the League. Players like Barkley said, "I don't just want to be in the league; I have to dominate the league." That's why he was worth three players combined. He was a winner, and he wanted to put a dent in the League.

Set goals high and monitor progress. Being realistic nev-er changed anything. Take your earnings or whatever you're working on and multiply that by 10, make it a goal, and be-lieve you can do it. You got to shoot for the moon; even if you miss, you will land among the stars. Always push yourself to do more. When Kobe Bryant decided that he wanted to be one of the best basketball players in the NBA, he went to see Michael Jordan. MJ understood something that most ath-letes don't understand. It would be best if you had a mindset of domination. As an athlete or business owner, you want to avoid competing with your opponents. Your goal should be total domination. You must dominate the field, own it, and that's what Kobe did. He works out four times a day as a basketball player, whereas most players work out twice a day the most. It might sound contrary to breeding positivity, and it will be if all you focus on are the outcomes of your attempts. Enjoy the journey along the way, and pay attention to what you're accomplishing instead of the target goal you set for yourself. It's the one time I suggest you look back in proportion to looking forward.

I'm a huge basketball fan. I love sports because I'm a very competitive guy. I love to watch the games live in the arenas or on TV. But during the regular NBA season, I barely watch the games. Each team has to play 82 games, so there's not that much intensity early in the season, especially before the All-Star game. So, I tend to watch to get a feel for the players and to put each team into perspective. But when the playoffs come, every player brings their A-game. Some players turn into Beast Mode; that's a win or go home because something is at stake. Every player is in the spotlight. You don't have other options when your back is against the wall. There is no plan B – it's a Plan A or nothing; that's when you become a different you, your mind is fully awake, and the pressure is on. The game is fun. I love to watch the playoffs because no player wants to go home. Everybody wants to win. Some players go above and beyond and do whatever it takes to win basketball games, to give it everything they have.

Tim Grover, Michael Jordan's trainer, wrote a book called Relentless. He was also the personal trainer for Dwayne Wade and Kobe Bryant. Attitude is a common word. It should be an all-the-time thing, but people who think they have a good one often slip at the first hint of trouble. The others, who maintain a good one with regularity, are likely to get help from attitude's brethren-of-the-faith variety. All will always turn out well if applied regularly.

Attitude is also similar to self-esteem. You have to build it on your own. How can you teach yourself to develop a winning attitude? It's all about how you think. You have to focus on things you can control. Give yourself a leg up by focusing on the things you love. It's much easier to develop a great attitude when doing something you love.

Get into the process and out of the outcome. Make sure you can commit. Setting high goals is only possible if you can commit to working toward and achieving them. This exercise also involves determining the things in your life you will need to sacrifice to achieve what you want. Make no excuses. You are a victim of your vibration. You are accountable for everything you do and everything that happens to you. Accept it. Own it.

Behavior plays a crucial part. Don't ever give up on being true to yourself. Winners quit. They quit the right things at the correct times. They also choose the right things to start and focus only on them. That's why you wouldn't consider thinking of them as quitters. If you've entangled yourself in something that isn't your passion, be true to yourself and find something else that is. It's your life. If you continue doing something you don't want to, you're only lying to yourself.

Relationships make the world go around. Surround yourself with the right people. You're the average of all the people you spend the most time with. Do the math. Relationships are meant to empower you and should never victimize you. Walk away if any connection isn't helping you become who you want to be. Be grateful. It's impossible to have a bad attitude when you have gratitude. Be thankful for everything you have because people will never have what you have today.

It's hard to fight someone willing to die on the battlefield. Bob Marley said, "You don't know how strong you are until being strong is your only choice." If you want something bad enough, you will find a way to get it. Burn the ship, leave yourself with no other option, no going back. Learn, learn and learn. Life will never get easier, but I assure you, you will get wiser.

Aim high because higher is waiting on you

Chapter 16

Stay hungry

Once, a man asked Socrates what's the secret to success. Socrates asked the man to meet him the following day and join him for his usual morning bath in the river. When the two men met, they walked deeper into the river. When the water was up to their neck, Socrates took the young man by surprise and dunked his head into the water. The man struggled to get his head out of the water, but Socrates kept him steady until the man's face started turning blue. A few moments later, Socrates released his head, and the man finally got out of the water, gasped, and took a deep breath.

"Why did you do that?" the man shouted.

"When you were in the water, what did you want the most?" Socrates asked.

"Air," the man replied.

"You asked me the secret to success. There is only one secret. When you want success as badly as you wanted the air, then you will get it." Socrates said.

Indeed, if our desire is weak, it will not produce great results.

Absolute desperation is beautiful. The most alive you will ever feel when you are the most desperate. In life, we are trying to avoid this all the time. I'm here to tell you to embrace it and seek the desperation. I would take hunger and desire over IQ, talent, skills, and knowledge any day of the week. I can teach you skills and lessons, but I can't give you heart, hunger, or desire. I can't teach you the courage to be desperate because desperate people look a little funny. Desperate people don't fit in. They stand out, and they get criticism. Most people would rather not stand out. They'd instead not leave their crew, instead not take the heat. Most people would say, "I would love to be a millionaire. I would love to win, have the best body, and have my dream relationship, to be happier, but I don't want to look bad doing it. I don't want to seem desperate. I don't want to look different. I don't want to step out of the crowd." If you are one of those people who are more worried about what other people would say about you than they are about genuinely winning, you will always be held back.

What is your level of hunger and desperation, and how bad do you want it? Do you need it like you need to breathe, eat, exist, and stay alive? Or do you just want it?

One of the most creative geniuses of the 20th century was once fired from a newspaper because he was told he lacked creativity. I'm glad he didn't listen. Trying to persevere, Disney formed his first animation company, Laugh-O-Gram Films. He had a deal with a New York distribution company to get his films into theaters. But in 1922, things went terribly wrong. The distributor began to cheat Disney out of his money, causing the new filmmaker to fall short of the funding needed to cover his finances. Faced with mounting debts and no money to pay his bills, Walt Disney filed for bankruptcy in 1923. Following the close of an important distributor partner. Disney was hungry, desperate, and out of money. He found his way to Hollywood and faced even more criticism and failure until, finally, his first few classic films started to skyrocket in popularity.

If it wasn't for his hunger and desperation to keep going, the world might have never known Mickey Mouse, Snow White, or any of the other extraordinary creations of Disney. For debtors who have a vision for their life and legacy, never hesitate to use bankruptcy as a tool to help you fulfill what you're destined to do in this world.

Tyler Perry has spoken publicly about his experiences with homelessness and how he lived in his car for several years while he was trying to make it as a playwright and actor in Atlanta. Despite facing numerous setbacks and challenges. Perry then transitioned to film and television, facing further obstacles such as criticism and limited resources and struggled to secure funding for his projects, leading him to often finance his own work. Despite these challenges, Perry persisted and utilized his unique perspective and storytelling to create successful and influential works, such as the "Madea" franchise and the television drama "The Haves and the Have Nots." His determination and hard work have made him one of the most successful producers in the entertainment industry. If movie producer Tyler Perry did not fight for his dreams, the world would never have been exposed to Oscar-winner Viola Davis and countless others.

Most people like their goals or outcomes but are not hungry for them. They need to be starving or desperate enough for them.

When you know why you want something and are desperate to get somewhere, you think more significantly and find new solutions. There's power in being desperate. It is something that most people avoid because they feel that desperation is a weakness. I am here to tell you that desperation is one of the most powerful emotions you can have because when you're desperate, you find a reserve and a reservoir of ideas, talents, and strengths that you did not know you had. Ironically, the one thing most people avoid in their life is hunger caused by desperation. When you are starving, you become desperate. Think about somebody living on the street. They're hungry and desperate to eat. How resourceful can you get if your children are starving and you have to feed them?

It's hard to repeat as a champion in sports because the challenger is hungrier for that title – someone who has never had it before but can taste it. Someone who knows that if they win that belt, their whole life will change – they will be the world champion, with all the endorsements and the money. Someone hungrier for that title, as opposed to someone just trying to hold on to a title, has much more desperation to win. That's why most of the time, the challenger beats the champion. It's hard to repeat as a champion because the hunger level decreases slightly.

Tom Bradys, Serena Williams, Kobe Bryant, Lebron James – all have a way of feeding their hunger all the time and increasing it. That's what separates them from the rest. It isn't just their work ethic or their talent. It isn't just their practice schedules. No, what separates them is that they're just hungrier. 99% of athletes lose their hunger as soon as they sign their first pro contract, their first championship, and their first significant amount of money. When the hunger is lost, the focus is gone.

How do you wake up in the morning?

Do you jump out of bed and look forward to starting the day? Do you wake up in the morning but don't want to get out of bed? Do you hear the alarm clock ring, but you press the snooze button repeatedly until you are forced to get up and go to the bathroom? Or wake up even more tired than when you went to bed?

What do you think about when you wake up?

Do you thik about everything you need to do and your endless to-do list and feel overwhelmed before you get out of bed?

Or

Do you wake up thinking about all the challenges you are facing, all the criticism people have given you, and the areas where you have not succeeded? So, when you feel discouraged and de-motivated.

Or

Do you think about what is missing in your life – not enough money, no big title after your name, no flashy car, and so on?

When faced with a problem, what do you do?

Do you spend time discussing and analyzing the problem in great depth and then defining it in unsolvable terms?

Or

Do you find someone else to blame?

The stress level in your life comes down to how much of life you feel like you control and how much this life controls you. Do you tend to take control more of what's happening, or are events controlling you? What you focus on dramatically affects your feelings, whether you're thriving or surviving. If you focus on what you can't control or what's missing from your life constantly, that focus pattern will make you frustrated, overwhelmed, and depressed. It won't even matter if you're taking anti-depressive meds. Focus equals power. If you want to thrive, you have to focus on what you can control. You have to focus on the difference you can make with what's already in your life that you're grateful for.

General Norman Schwarzkopf, during the time he was commanding U.S. forces, would go to the Desert Storm conflict, as they called it in those days. He was just a brilliant army officer who came out of West Point. He was asked where he developed his decision-making capability. He said when he was young, he was an assistant to an Army General. There was a research project with the Pentagon to decide which way the defense department would move toward the future and how it would operate. It was a very strategic decision, with arguments on all sides. It went back and forth for five years, and nothing was resolved. They eventually came to the general that Schwarzkopf was helping them decide. They had a one-hour meeting scheduled. After twenty minutes, the general stood up and picked one of the two options, and said, do that!! He did it with absolute certainty. He saluted the others at the meeting and walked out of the meeting.

Schwarzkopf said he was curious to know how the general could make a decision like that. There were loads and loads of research, and he knew the general had yet to read all of it. Schwarzkopf finally went to him and asked how he decided which direction to go for the Armed Services when he didn't have all the information. The general replied that no one had all the information. And since no one had decided in five years, he decided to put all the resources in one of the directions and to see what would happen. If he were wrong, they would discover that quicker than sitting on the fence for the next five years trying to make a decision.

Leadership is making decisions. If you're going to lead your own life, you must make decisions. Schwarzkopf said he realized rule number one in life is when you're put in command, take charge, and make a decision. You'll find out quicker than sitting around arguing if it's right or wrong. The exciting thing is that the more you make decisions, the better you get at them. What makes somebody a leader is their willingness to make decisions that other people won't make. You do have to put yourself on the line, knowing that you're going to be wrong in some of those decisions, but you're going to find out quickly what works so that you can adapt and change your approach to still get where you want to go. Be decisive. If you don't like your body, change it; if you don't like your relationship, change it. Start by changing yourself. Indecision is the enemy of progress.

Hunger for success is a vital aspect of achieving one's goals. This drive and determination should be cultivated in a friendly and active way. By setting clear and achievable objectives, taking consistent and focused actions toward them, and surrounding oneself with supportive and motivated individuals, one can harness the power of their hunger for success to accomplish great things. Remember that success is about achieving material wealth and finding fulfillment and satisfaction in one's personal and professional pursuits. By maintaining a strong hunger for success and a positive attitude, anything is possible. Don't be afraid to dream big, set clear and achievable goals, stay focused and active, and never let setbacks bring you down. Keep that hunger alive, stay motivated and go out there and make it happen!

Chapter 17

Giving unconditionally

Robert Ford, aka Rocky, and J.B. Moore were two workers at Billboard looking to establish themselves as record producers in the eighties. So, they hooked up with the young Kurtis Blow, a rapper from Harlem. They spent $2,000, which represented all their savings, into recording and then pressing a single with him called "Christmas Rappin'." But Rocky and J.B. needed help figuring out how to create a buzz around Kurtis, so they enlisted Russell Simmons to help them. Russell was happy to take on the job. He was just a party promoter at that time, but when he listened to "Christmas Rappin'," he knew Kurtis had the potential to be a major artist.

It would have been easy to create a buzz if Kurtis were a rock 'n' roller or a soul singer. But going directly to the labels to shop for a deal for Kurtis would have been a dead-end because back then, Polygram Records, one of the biggest labels, thought that hip hop was nothing more than a novelty whose days were numbered. So instead of wasting time with the record labels trying to sell them on Kurtis, Russell started to give away copies of "Christmas Rappin'" to whomever he thought might play it. Russell gave it to D.J.s at famous Manhattan and the Bronx clubs, Rooftops, Small Paradise in Harlem, Disco Fever, the Loft, and Frankie Crocker at WBLS, who was the hottest radio personality in the city at the time. He gave copies away to everybody and anybody until there were no more left, but that strategy worked like a charm. A few D.J.s started playing it, and after the crowd went nuts every time it came on, word spread fast that "Christmas Rappin'" was a hot record.

Then Russell, Rocky, and J.B. pressed up new versions of the record with an order number from Polygram Records on it. As the song started getting even more and more spins, the records stores started calling up Polygram, asking to order copies of "Christmas Rappin'." Obviously, Polygram had no idea what the store was talking about but seeing heavy demand for the record; they managed to track them down and sign Kurtis to a deal (the first for a rapper with a major label). The records went on to sell more than 500,000 copies. If the record hadn't been given away, the D.J.s wouldn't have heard it, let alone play it, and if the D.J.s hadn't played it in the influential clubs, the stores wouldn't have ordered it, and if the stores hadn't ordered it, Polygram would never have given Kurtis a deal. Giving from the beginning, however, is what turned those dreams into reality.

Back then, it was tough to promote your talent, to show society what you could do or how good you could rap, sing, play, or whatever your talent was. That was before the internet and social network came into play. Nowadays, record labels go on YouTube looking for artists. Millions of talented artists were found there because they shared their talent by uploading videos of themselves singing or playing instruments. Those artists were ready to show the world how talented they are

Dr. King said, "Life's most persistent and urgent question is what are you doing for others." No one has ever become poor by giving. We make a living by what we get and make a life by what we give. The happiest people are not those that get more but those that give more. Giving is the essence of life. They say life is like a game of tennis – those who don't serve well end up losing.

Each of us has a unique gift we would like to share with the world, but the question is how to get that gift out of the heart and into the world where it can be loved and appreciated.

The Canadian singer Justin Bieber was raised by a single mother in Ontario, Canada. As a child, he learned to play the drums, the piano, the guitar, and the trumpet. In

2007, he participated in a local singing competition, placing second, and his mother posted a video of his performance on YouTube for friends and family who could not attend. She later uploaded other homemade videos in which Bieber sang popular rhythm and blues (R&B) songs and occasionally accompanied himself on acoustic guitar. Those videos soon attracted attention beyond their originally intended audience. Among those who saw Bieber was Scooter Braun, a music promoter and talent agent, who invited the 13-year-old to record a demo tape at a studio in Atlanta. While there, Bieber encountered R&B singer Usher and arranged an informal audition with him. Impressed by Bieber's natural confidence and vocal talent, Usher helped sign him to a recording contract in 2008, and the rest is history.

How many talents got found on YouTube? How did people get rich off YouTube? They decided to share their talents with the world, showcase their work, teach, answer questions, and help others grow their talent. YouTube rewards them. I love YouTube, with billions of videos showing how to do pretty much anything. I learned tons of stuff on YouTube. I earned money because of YouTube and some skills I learned and then shared how to do them even better.

I believe that God is in each of us, so when I give you something that helps you or puts a smile on your face, I feel like God will reward me for that. The act of giving triggers the receiving. Focus on giving, and the receiving will take care of itself. I love to make people smile.

First of all, a smile is contagious. You give a smile, and you get a smile. Give away the things that you love the most and see what happens. If you love to be happy, try giving happiness away, and much joy will come rushing toward you. What goes around always comes around.

Dr. Karl Menninger, a famous psychiatrist, was asked what he would advise a person to do if he felt a nervous breakdown coming on. People expected him to reply to go consult a psychiatrist. He said to their astonishment, "Leave your home. Go across the railroad tracks. Find someone in need and do something to help that person." By helping enough people get what they want, you will get what you want," said Zig Ziglar. . It can't be all about you all the time.

A life lived for others is the way to live," as Helen Keller said. An excellent way to forget your troubles is to help others out of their troubles – the givers always receive. Always look for ways to give, to add value to other people. Giving is the ultimate way to find yourself. Sometimes it's hard to give when you need to be given. Bills are piling up, paycheck is already allocated, no money in the bank, and helping someone is the last thing on your mind. That's when you start exercising your giving or sharing muscle. Losing yourself in helping others will help you to shift your mindset. What you focus on always expands. By focusing on what you're giving, more giving thoughts will be produced, which will help you recover quickly.

Focusing on the problems and being in your bubble all

day will wear you out. It's like holding a cup of water for a few hours. For the first few minutes, a cup feels light. However, with every other minute, it becomes heavier and heavier. The mind functions better when it's at play, not when stressed out—not thinking about the problem; that's how you fix the problem. Muscles grow during rest, not during exercise.

I am a big tipper when I go to restaurants; I usually find the waiter cool and polite. I often try to give them a big tip, but then my friends object. They used to tell me how absurd it was for me to give the waiter a big tip because the service was not even good, the waiter took too long to bring our food or was not very polite, and so on. I love to put a smile on their faces because I've had jobs like that before, not exactly as a waiter, but when a generous guest would give me a tip, sometimes a big tip, it makes me happy and appreciated. And I just wanted them to feel the same way." And you know what? More money always finds a way back into my pocket.

Nowadays, everyone is hustling and trying to make it, but how can you ensure that you will get what you want out of the gift that God gave you? How can you find that designer to design your artwork, that label company to promote your music, and that investor to invest in you? First, you have to give your talent away, share it, teach it online for free, and showcase your work.

Refrain from covering up your ideas. Do you remember from school other students preventing you from seeing their answers by placing their arm around their exercise book or exam paper? Some people are so secretive with their ideas. They think they shouldn't share them because someone might take the credit. The problem with hoarding is you end up living off your reserves, and eventually, you'll become stale. If you give everything, you are left with nothing, forcing you to look, be aware, and replenish. Somehow the more you give away, the more comes back to you. Ideas are open knowledge, don't claim ownership.

When we focus on the needs of others, we can let go of our own egocentric tendencies and gain a sense of purpose and fulfillment. Lack will also amplify itself when you focus on it. That energy will create more energy just alike. When you focus on giving, the universe will sense that energy and keep feeding you with the same energy to keep giving. Giving away ourselves can help us find ourselves. By committing to the needs of others, we are able to gain a deeper understanding of our own values, priorities, and humanity. Through acts of kindness, empathy, or service, we can positively impact the world, and in the process, we can discover the best version of ourselves.

Chapter 18

Take in the Good

We realized we needed carrots to complete our soup on our way home from the Garden City movie theater. Since it was past midnight and most stores were closed, we drove to our old neighborhood to buy some. A young Spanish clerk charged us a dollar for a small carrot. Although we knew it was overpriced, we paid for it anyway. We complained about the store overcharging us and how these stores take advantage of people in these neighborhoods. However, I then reminded my wife that we should be grateful that the store was open and had carrots available for us to buy. Instead of focusing on the negative and complaining, we should appreciate that we were able to find what we needed.

If you had an evaluation at work, your manager said that you did a fantastic job all year long, gave you a good review on your performance, noted that you are such a good employee and a tremendous asset to the company, and so on, and then mentioned few areas that you need to work on to improve, guess where your mind will be once you finish your evaluation? It will be all over the things that the manager said you needed to work on. If out of 100 questions, you get two wrong, your mind will dwell on those two wrongs and forget about the rest.

Our brains are like Teflon for positive experiences. We don't easily remember positive thoughts; however, our brains are like Velcro for bad or negative thoughts that tend to stick to our brains and are hard to get off.

If I mention Bill Clinton's name, most people immediately think of Monica Lewinsky. However, it is unfortunate that this association overshadows his presidency's positive actions and accomplishments. Despite these controversies, many Americans believe that Clinton was one of the best presidents in history due to his achievements in office. Unfortunately, his reputation is tarnished by his association with Monica Lewinsky.

What do you usually think about at the end of the day: the 50 positive experiences you had or the one negative interaction? Like the guy who cut you off in traffic, what do you wish you had said differently to a co-worker or the one thing on your To Do list that didn't get done? Research suggests that it takes five positive interactions to make up for a single negative interaction in a relationship; the same is true of self-talk.

Couples often argue, using phrases such as "You ain't nothing. I've put up with your sorry ass for all these years. I can't stand you. You're a real piece of crap," despite being married for over 20 years. In the heat of the argument, all the positive aspects of the relationship, such as gifts, vacations, surprises, and taking care of the family and kids, are forgotten. Eventually, one partner apologizes and asks for forgiveness, saying, "I'm so sorry. I didn't mean to say those things."

We are built with a greater sensitivity to the negative than the positive. Therefore, most of us can have a relatively good day filled with multiple positive experiences yet will still allow a single negative one to take more of our attention and keep us dwelling on the future or the past, thinking about what we are going to do or what we should have done. We need a mindful, active process of taking in the positive to compensate for our brain's negative wiring.

We need to change our thinking toward absorbing the good. So, instead of positive experiences washing through you like water through a sieve, they'll collect in implicit memory deep down in your brain. Science says, "Neurons that fire together wire together." The more you get your neurons firing about positive facts, the more they'll be wiring up positive neural structures.

Taking in the good is a brain-science-savvy and psychologically skillful way to improve your feelings, get things done, and treat others. It is among the top five personal growth methods I know. In addition to being suitable for adults, it's great for children, helping them to become more resilient, confident, and happy. Mindfulness or awareness is one strategy we can use to take in the positive. Often, we just need to pause to enjoy ourselves and remember the positive things that happen.

Here's how to take in the good – in three simple steps.

1. Look for good facts and turn them into good experiences.

Taking a moment to appreciate the good things in life can make a big difference in your overall well-being. Whether savoring a delicious cup of coffee or receiving an unexpected compliment, take note of positive events and aspects of the world and yourself. Try to do this at least a few times a day, which only takes a few seconds. You can do it privately, in your daily life, or during special moments of reflection. It's a great way to end the day just before falling asleep, as your brain is particularly receptive to new learning.

Identify and challenge thoughts or feelings that impede your ability to experience pleasure, such as believing that you do not deserve it or feeling good is selfish or vain. Let go of the belief that feeling good will leave you vulnerable to negative events.

Barriers to feeling good are common and understandable – but they get in the way of taking in the resources you need to feel better, have more strength, and have more inside to give to others. So, acknowledge them to yourself, and then turn your attention to the good news. Keep opening up to it, breathing and relaxing, letting the good facts affect you.

It's like sitting down to a meal: don't just eat it – enjoy it!

2. Enjoy the experience.

Most of the time, a good experience is mild, and that's fine. But try to stay with it for 20 or 30 seconds in a row – instead of getting distracted by something else. As you do that, sense that it is filling your body, becoming a rich experience. As Marc Lewis and other researchers have shown, the longer something is held in awareness, and the more emotionally stimulating it is, the more neurons fire and thus wire together, and the stronger this experience lasts in your memory.

You are not craving or clinging to positive experiences since that would ultimately lead to tension and disappointment. You are doing the opposite: by taking them in and filling yourself up with them, you will increasingly feel less fragile or needy inside and less dependent on external supplies. Your happiness and love will become more unconditional, based on an inner fullness rather than on whether the momentary facts in your life happen to be good ones.

3. Intend and sense that the good experience is sinking into you.

People sense good experiences in different ways. Some feel it in their body like a warm glow spreading through their chest or like the warmth of a cup of hot cocoa on a cold wintry day. Others visualize things like golden syrup sinking inside, bringing good feelings and soothing old places of hurt, filling in old holes of loss or yearning; a child might imagine a jewel going into a treasure chest in her heart. And some might know conceptually that while this good experience is held in awareness, its neurons are firing busily away and gradually wiring together.

When you're fully in the present, your thoughts or worries disappear. Humans are rarely in the present, wandering between the past and the future. I am active in meditation, yoga, jogging, and lifting weights. It helps me quiet that negative voice that is always talking non-stop. I keep a daily journal, morning and evening, to help me evaluate the day positively and negatively, noting things that I need to work on and that I need to pat myself on the back and congratulate myself. When you're present, you're mindful. That's when you are able to choose. You can be negative or positive at that point. When your brain wanders, you are most likely tending to be negative. I practice "savoring" the positive experiences at the end of the day. I take time each day to be mindful of positive experiences. It is not about putting a happy shiny face on everything or turning away from the hard things in life. It's about nourishing inner well-being, contentment, and peace – refuges to which you can always return.

Staying present in the moment can help clear your mind of worries and negative thoughts. It's natural for humans to often wander between the past and future, but practicing mindfulness through activities such as meditation, yoga, jogging, and weightlifting can help quiet that inner voice that can be critical and negative. I Keep a daily journal to reflect on the day's positive and negative experiences to help me focus on what I need to work on and what I should celebrate. When you're present and mindful, you have the power to choose to focus on the positive or negative. One way to cultivate a positive outlook is to practice "savoring" positive experiences at the end of the day. Take the time to focus on the good things that happened. It's about nourishing inner well-being, contentment, and peace and creating a refuge to which you can always return. I have always dreamed of having a TV channel that will only broadcast positive news, mainly achievements, inspirational stories, people doing great, innovators, dreamers, people who want to change the world with their ideas, good parenting, and so on to inspire others to do good. I had a friend who always loved sending me negative videos through WhatsApp, like people suffering and dying – pure negative bias. I told her to stop looking for the negative news all the time and send me some achievements, some positive news, something inspirational. She did that several times and then returned to the negative news again. I had to block her and stop talking to her. It's essential to surround yourself with positivity and avoid negativity as much as possible, whether in the form of social media or negative-minded friends.

When life gets overwhelming, and you're feeling stressed out, channeling your energy into a fun hobby can be a great way to shift your focus from the negative to the positive. I love to spend time in my shop, working on various projects. I easily lose track of time because there's always something to do. Building and creating something is really satisfying and helps me take my mind off any stressors. Having a hobby is a great way to relax and de-stress; it's a perfect way to shift your focus on something else.

I've been taking classes to learn fun skills like using a sewing machine, making ice cream, bagels, bread, and even Vietnamese nems and cakes. I do all of this not only to improve my skills but also to feel good about myself. Instead of buying gifts for people, I like to make them something special; it's more personal. I love seeing the look of surprise on their faces and hearing them say, "Wow, you made this? You're so talented; how did you learn to do this? Will you teach me?" I really enjoy sharing my skills and teaching others.

Another critical thing to keep in mind is to pursue work that you're genuinely passionate about. When you're doing something you love, your job won't feel like a chore, and you won't mind spending most of your day doing it.

Maintaining contentment with oneself is crucial. Recently, an anonymous quote struck me deeply: "God won't visit you if you aren't content." Regardless of current emotions, preserving a grateful attitude and being thankful for life's gift is imperative. Every day above ground is a wonderful day. Emphasize on life's positive aspects because what you concentrate on grows.

Chapter 19

Health: The Ultimate Wealth

On June 24th, 2020, I accomplished a huge milestone: running 3000 miles! When I started, I couldn't even run one mile without feeling exhausted. But I knew I needed to improve my health and make running a daily habit. So, I set a small goal: to run just one mile every day for 21 days. Starting small is the best way to build a habit, and at first, it felt ridiculous for someone my size to only run one mile a day. But I stuck with it, knowing that the goal was to establish a consistent routine rather than improve my running immediately. And it worked! Once I had that routine in place, I gradually improved my distance. So, if you're starting to work on your health, remember to build a consistent routine first, and then you'll be able to progress and achieve bigger goals."

"Building a habit takes around 3 to 5 weeks, so I increased my distance after three weeks. Every week, I added a mile to my run until I reached my goal of running 5 miles daily. I run at least 5 miles daily from Monday to Friday and 15 miles on Saturday and Sunday, averaging 45 miles per week."

Running every day is a non-negotiable. My wife and even my mom expressed concern that I might wear myself out or harm my knees, ankles, or back. They asked why I was training like I was running a marathon around the world. I was getting a lot of negativity from them about my daily 5-mile runs. They thought I was crazy, and I even started hiding to run to avoid their criticism. But one day, while browsing magazines at Barnes & Noble bookstore, I came across an article about a 59-year-old woman named Catra Corbet from Fremont, California. She runs at least 80 miles per week and has logged 79,543 since 1996. She has also run 220 Ultramarathons and 100 miles in 21 hours and 20 minutes. People told me I was insane for running 5 miles a day when in comparison, Catra had run 80,000 miles between 1996 to 2015, averaging 80 miles per week. I was only averaging 40 miles per week. This realization made me understand that I should be hanging out with people like Catra to push me to do more instead of allowing my intellectual property to be polluted by small-minded people's opinions."

As a runner, I know something that others don't: the feeling after a run is the most blissful thing you can ever feel.

You'll never hear someone regret working out. People don't regret going to the gym, kickboxing, or strength training. These activities make you feel good and accomplished. By pushing yourself to do the right thing, the best time to do it is in the morning."

I try to get it out of the way in the morning because most gyms are crowded at night or after work. Soon as I get up, exercising is the first thing I focus on. I turn to my Nike App to keep up with my progress.

Recently, I've been starting my day at 5 AM by praying, reading, and then heading outside for a run. After my run, I take some time to stretch and cool down with a 20-minute meditation. Then, I sit down at my computer and finish writing my book. I am most inspired and comfortable working in my bathroom, where I spend most of my time reading and meditating. Some people may find it strange that I spend so much time in the bathroom, but I even considered turning it into my home office. My wife wasn't too thrilled about the idea of building a bookshelf in the guest bathroom, though! just a thought.

Everyone knows that working out, running, kickboxing, jogging, and playing sports are some of the best investments of our time. I like to brag sometimes and tell people that I run 5 miles daily. I even mentioned it recently during a job interview, and my employer was impressed by my dedication. I told him I'd been committed to running 5 miles daily at 6 AM for over three years. He was shocked and said he could never do something like that. After that conversation, I knew I had the job in the bag because he could see how dedicated I am to taking care of myself."

I remember one Sunday Evening, as I sat on my couch watching TV, a couple of chubby doctors appeared on the screen and shared their advice on running. They warned that running five times a day would be detrimental to your knees and urged people not to run every day. But something about their advice didn't sit well with me. I couldn't help but think of Kobe Bryant and Michael Jordan, two of the greatest athletes of all time. They worked out intensively, 3 to 4 times a day for almost 20 years, and their knees were perfectly fine. They were examples of how consistent and intense workouts can benefit the body.

I realized that it's important to remember that you can't take advice from someone who hasn't done something similar to what you're doing. It's common sense, but it's not always common practice. I can't take advice from an overweight Doctor or a personal trainer who's not fit. You have to practice what you preach.

When you start on a journey to be healthy, don't focus too much on the destination. What I mean by that is you might be overweight right now, and you want to lose 40 lbs or more. So it's very daunting to look at yourself in the mirror because your brain tells you, "that's impossible; let's not kid ourselves, you've been overweight most of your life; this is who you are; it's the same thing to ask someone to eat an elephant, that's a humongous task." Focusing on the destination might be very discouraging. Focus on an action you can do daily, and you will reach your goal over time. When I said that I wanted to run 3000 miles, it was a scary goal for me. But I did not focus on the end goal. I focused on what I could do in a single day. I had limited time every day, so I devoted myself to spending one hour a day on that goal, so in one hour, I knew I could run 5 miles. I ran 5 miles a day for three years. It took time, but I achieved that goal. It does not matter how small your steps are. As long as you don't stop, you will get there.

My friend had a dream of becoming fitter. He knew the journey would be challenging but determined to make it happen. He reached out to me to join him on his journey. We decided to jog and kickbox every day, hoping to shed some pounds and get in shape. We were dedicated and committed to our plan.

He started to weigh himself daily, eagerly awaiting the results of his hard work. But as the days passed, he noticed that the scale wasn't budging. He became discouraged and upset that all his effort wasn't yielding any results. He began to doubt his ability to achieve his dream.

But I reminded him that true success takes time and effort. I shared with him the wisdom of Tony Robbins, who said it's not about ability but motivation, drive, and burning desire to achieve something. I encouraged him to stay consistent with his daily actions and be patient with his progress. I reminded him that the key to success is to find his motivation and drive to achieve his goals, whether it's to be healthy, prosperous, or happy. As Simon Sinek said in his book, start with the why, not the how. When you have a strong reason why you should do something, you can bear any how.

Despite the initial disappointment, my friend didn't give up. He pushed through and continued to jog and kickboxing with me daily. He shifted his focus from the scale to the daily actions that he knew he should do. And eventually, his hard work paid off. He lost the weight he wanted and felt happier and healthier than ever.

My friend's journey teaches us that even if others think it's impossible if you have a strong enough motivation, you'll find a way to make it happen. Don't let anything stand in your way. Stay consistent, be patient, and let the results care for themselves.

I am my Doctor; I have a daily menu that I follow every day to keep me energized. I manage my energy because, without energy, I can't do much. You can be the most intelligent man on the planet, but your intelligence becomes useless if you are always exhausted and tired. After a workout, I used to eat pancakes, French toast, and so on. I used to be dead tired and ready to knock out. I switched to fruits until noon. I got that from Jesse Itzler's book "Living with a seal." He eats fruits until noon to stay energized.

One of the most common sayings in Japan is "Hara Ha-chi bu," which is repeated before and after eating and means something like "fill your belly to 80%". Ancient wisdom advises against eating until you are full. Okinawa is located in Northern Japan, where the world's longest-living people live. Okinawans stop eating when they feel their stomachs reach 80 percent of their capacity, rather than overeating and wearing down their bodies with a long digestive process that accelerates cellular oxidation. In Islam, you should divide your stomach into 3: one filled with food, one with water, and one empty. A stomach loaded with food absorbs the power of the attention needed for the performance.

Metabolism slows down 90 percent after 30 minutes of sitting. The enzymes that move the bad fat from your arteries to your muscles, where it can get burned off, slow down. And after 2 hours, good cholesterol drops 20 percent. Just getting up for minutes is going to get things going again. These ideas are so simple they're almost stupid, says Gavin Bradley in a 2015 interview with the Washington Post. Bradley is one of the preeminent experts on the subject and the director of an international organization dedicated to building awareness of how detrimental sitting all the time can be to our help.

Here are a few tips on how to increase your energy level.

1. Establish a routine that provides adequate eight hours of sleep, sufficient exercise, and proper nutrition while nurturing your professional and personal relationships. As you

incorporate energy-boosting strategies into your daily routine, they will become habitual, creating an endless energy source that schedule changes, weather, or other distractions won't disrupt.

2. Proper nutrition is at the absolute center of your energy levels. Junk food, processed items, and sugar make you feel lethargic and can lead to weight gain. If you need more energy, you must embrace a sustainable and healthy diet that includes low-toxicity foods, purified water, and essential oils to jump-start your process of learning how to increase energy naturally

3. Following a healthy diet is pivotal for those who want to increase energy levels, but even the most well-planned diet has gaps. High-quality supplements can fill those gaps with nutrients your body needs to thrive and increase energy while improving overall health, whether you are trying to lose weight, gain muscle, or need more energy.

4. Movement leads to more energy in the long run and is one of the most important physical ways to increase energy. Exercising 30 minutes a day for at least three days each week benefits all bodily systems while facilitating high-quality sleep and increasing energy levels. If you can't manage this level of exercise, start with 10 or 15 minutes of walking or light weights a couple of days a week and work your way up. If you need extra help, consider working with a health

coach to develop an effective exercise plan.

5. Letting your emotions control every action can be energy-draining and detrimental to creating healthy relationships. Therefore, learning how to control your feelings is a pivotal component of learning how to increase energy. Take control of your emotions today by paying attention to them and to what limiting beliefs they may indicate. By identifying triggers and letting go of the past, you can become the master of your own emotions and fill yourself with positive energy.

6. Those who look for ways to increase energy are sometimes beaten down by life. They often ask, "Why is this happening to me?" and feel they will never catch a break. A key to increasing energy levels is to look at life as if it's happening for you, not to you. That's a big difference. Instead of viewing events as failures or setbacks, look at them as necessary steps to creating the person you're meant to be. That's the price you have to pay to get what you want.

7. Studies from the blue Zone suggest that people who live longest are not the ones who do the most exercise but rather the ones who move the most.

Being healthy, exercising, and having energy are all interconnected and crucial for leading a fulfilling life. Regular exercise improves physical health and mental well-being and can increase energy levels. By making healthy choices, such as eating a balanced diet and getting enough sleep, we can further enhance our ability to exercise and feel energized. Remember, it's never too late to start making positive changes in our health and fitness. With small steps and consistent effort, we can improve our overall health and well-being and live the life we deserve with energy and vitality.

Chapter 20

Getting what you want

Would you like to win the lotto?

Of course, who wouldn't?

So why don't you buy a ticket?

I don't need to be a psychologist to tell you why you don't buy lotto tickets. It's because you don't expect to win, and given the odds of winning the lottery, that might seem like a reasonable conclusion. It's very important to understand that you've always acted based on what you expected, not what you wanted. What you want and what you expect are completely different things. An expectation is a belief about whether or not you will get what you want.

There are lots of things that you want but that you can't quite seem to obtain. No matter how hard you try to create change, you often stay stuck because expectation + action = the creation of your life's experiences. It might be surprising to know that most people go about their day-to-day lives thinking about acting on what they want, but in reality, they act on their expectations.

I was reading about a renowned psychologist Jenny Williams in Denver. She said that one of her clients, Maggy, a gorgeous and successful woman, was very shy and had a history of picking the wrong man. Maggy had recently gotten out of a bad marriage and decided that she was ready to meet someone new. And so, she decided that she would try online dating, but she was having bad date after bad date. The men did not look like their pictures. They often forget their wallet. Some of them did not show up at all. One day Maggy came into the psychologist's office and immediately burst into tears. "I had the awful date in my life," she cried. "He was amazing and absolutely everything I have been looking for in a man, but I completely blew it. I was so certain it would be another bad date and a waste of time that I told him to meet me for coffee after my exercise class. I did not have time to shower, so I showed up in my gym clothes, all sweaty and with no makeup. But there he was, mister immaculately groomed, tall and handsome, perfect smile. I was so mortified and self-conscious that I could not even make eye contact. I just sat there, staring at the ground, laughing nervously. Finally, I told him I had to put more money in the parking meter, and then I left without even saying goodbye."

Maggy acted on what she expected – another bad date – and did not expect to meet a great guy. "I wish I could say that this kind of behavior is uncommon," the Doctor wrote, "but it's not. Having been in practice for more than ten years, one of the things she hears most often is, 'I want to change my life, but I don't believe that I can.' It seems people give up on their marriages, health, careers, and give up entirely because they don't think they can get what they want and are unwilling to try."

You may want something in your life, but you are not sure you can obtain it, so you are holding back. You take yourself out of the game when you don't act on what you want. Buying that lottery ticket does not guarantee winning, but not buying one does guarantee losing. You might be wondering why you do this. Our brains work on the principle of anticipation. We constantly predict what we think is likely to happen before it ever occurs. If you are walking in the park and hear a barking behind, you anticipate seeing a dog when you turn around. So you know that you need to be careful not to provoke a dog for aggression. As soon as you start to anticipate any event, you begin to feel and act in ways that will help you to prepare for what you think is going to happen. If your spouse has ever said to you, "We need to talk," then you know exactly what I mean. When you prepare for something that has not happened yet, you participate in the creation of the outcome; in other words, you create the self-fulfillment prophecy, just like Maggy felt anxious before her date, then she acted on what she expected, not what she wanted. She got what she expected – another bad date.

One of the reasons that our expectations can keep us so stuck is that we have an automatic tendency to use the past to predict the future – if you fail once, you think that you might fail again. When you think about the future, some part of the brain gets activated and makes you think about the past. However, just because you use the past to make predictions does not mean that your past is what's holding you back. What was holding Maggy back was not her past. It was that she did not believe that her future could be better than her past, and without that belief, she could not create something better, even when an opportunity presented itself right in front of her. If you are aware of your expectations in a particular situation, you can use your conscious mind to override the automatic thinking and plan to create a different outcome.

If Maggy had planned her date to go well, things might have turned out differently. Our expectations, along with our ability to get what we want, have a very profound impact on our emotional well-being. A large part of our brain is dedicated to anticipating rewards. J. R. Tolkien said, "A single dream is more powerful than a thousand realities." When you expect to get a reward, you feel a positive emotion, like happiness or joy. When you expect you will not get what you want, you feel sadness and disappointment, maybe even depression. The more significant the gap between what you expect and what you want, the more stress you feel.

So, what do you do when what you want does not match what you expect? There are only two ways you can feel good in this situation:

You can give up on what you want. Tell yourself that it's not worth the effort, that you did not want it anyway.

You can change your expectation to match what you want so that you can take action that is consistent with what you want.

So, how do you do the second? I will give you three simple steps to help you shift your expectations. Imagine an upcoming or future event – a goal you are trying to achieve, a work presentation, a holiday event with your family, or whatever.

Step 1 is asking yourself:

How is what I am expecting making me feel?

If you expect something positive, you will feel good about it. There is no need to fix positive emotions. But if you are expecting something you don't want, you will feel negative emotions like anxiety, fear, dread, and being overwhelmed.

Step 2 is asking yourself: What would I like to happen instead? This question identifies what you do want in this situation. What you want is often the very thing that you are not expecting. Remember, you want to win the lottery but don't expect to.

Step 3 is asking yourself: What do I need to do to get what I want to happen? When you have a negative expectation about a future event, it's because you focus on all the things that could go wrong. You are not generating thoughts and ideas about how to make it go right. Your assessment of the situation starts to change when your plan is laid out in front of you to get what you want. You begin to see the possibilities. This is where the shift happens. Every successful action you take toward that plan starts to change your expectations.

Maggy's psychologist wrote, "Now I realize that some of you readers might be thinking, 'I don't think this will work for me.' Several years ago, I might not have expected that such a simple process could make a difference in people's lives. I was working with a very depressed person for about six months. We had done so much work together, and nothing seemed to make any difference. One day I asked him, 'Where is the light at the end of the tunnel?' He looked at me with one of the blankest stares I had ever seen. Ever since that day, I have asked all my patients the same question, and most of them look at me the same way. They did not dare to dream how their life could be different because they did not believe it was possible. So, I started to change the focus of my work to almost exclusively helping my patients shift their expectations so they could find the light at the end of the tunnel. Five years of research showed that changing your expectations can significantly improve your life. The person mentioned earlier quit his dead-end job to start his successful company," said the Doctor

When you are motivated by what you want, change is possible. Remember the words of Henry Ford? He said, "Whether you think you can or can't, you are right." Your past isn't what defines who you are and where you are going; your expectation of the future limits you the most. Here's the good news: you can choose. You can decide to take action based on what you want. And when you do that, you allow yourself to step out of the past and create the life you truly want to live.

Getting what you want is not so easy. It could cost you a lot of money. I have always tried to get some business going with my shop and other things I do for people, but I can't seem to make much money at it. Should I say that I set my expectations too low, or was I expecting exactly what I got from customers?

When I opened my sign shop in Hempstead, I did not set any goals. I did not know how much I wanted to make by the hour. I did not define what my role in the business was. I had a friend there, an old classmate, and we were running the business. We could have been successful if what we wanted and expected had been the same. We did not expect much, so we did not get much, but we wanted to get much more than what we got. We did not believe we could get it, so we acted according to our beliefs. I would come to work when I felt like it. I did not define a timetable for the business, and that led to getting exactly what we expected, not much.

That's why in business or anything you want to bring into your life, it's 90% mental and 10% strategy. Tony Robbins said resourcefulness is the ultimate resource. The Merriam-Webster dictionary defines resourcefulness as the ability to meet challenging situations, create inventive ways to deal with a problem, find resources, and devise ways and means to keep moving. Believing that you can get what you want will put you in the right mindset and give you the right attitude.

We human beings have unlimited potential. If you believe that you can get what you want in life, your actions will match your beliefs, and you will get the results you want.

But, on the other hand, if you expect your life to change, but you don't really believe it can change for the better, your actions will match that belief, and you will do less. So, your results will suffer, and those results will keep you in a downward spiral, reinforcing those beliefs that it will never work.

But, on the other hand, if you expect your life to change, but you don't really believe it can change for the better, your actions will match that belief, and you will do less. So, your results will suffer, and those results will keep you in a downward spiral, reinforcing those beliefs that it will never work.

How many people act against themselves? Someone said, "You are your worst enemy," and that's true. Les Brown, the motivational speaker, says, "If there is no enemy within, the enemy outside can't do us any harm. We sabotage our own success."

I strongly believe that until you define what you want and expect the best outcome possible for your life, your business, or your relationship, you won't make any progress. What you truly want and what you expect has to be on the same frequency in order for them to be materialized.

Conclusion

This book has aimed to inspire and empower you to raise your standards, become the best version of yourself, and make a meaningful impact on the world. By reflecting on the lives and actions of individuals such as Mother Teresa, Mandela, Martin Luther King, and Rosa Parks, you have been reminded that one person can truly make a difference. You have been reminded that you, too, have unique gifts to offer the world, whether it's through writing a book, creating art, developing business ideas, or serving others in your own unique way.

But I know it can be scary to put yourself out there and live your vision. You may be thinking, "What if I fail? What if I'm not good enough?" That's why I want to remind you of Steve Jobs' wise words, "Remembering that you're going to die is the best way I know to avoid the trap of thinking you have something to lose. You're already naked. There is no reason not to follow your heart."

In other words, don't let the fear of failure or the unknown hold you back from living your purpose and sharing your gifts with the world. Instead, embrace the boldness that lies within you and dare to live your vision. Because when you do, you'll be amazed at how much you can accomplish and how much you can inspire others to do the same.

So, my dear friends, I encourage you to be bold, to take action, and to "die empty" by giving your all to the world. The world needs your gifts right now, so don't wait any longer. Go out there and make a difference. You got this!

Acknowlegments

It would be impossible to more than scratch the surface in the form of acknowledgments to the many individuals who have helped me through the years. However, some have contributed so much that their names literally jump off the pages of my life and demand recognition. Heading to the list is my mom Fatou Diakhate who never stopped supporting me. She invested in my education, sent me to the USA to finish my degree, coached me through the years, and was my number one Fan. Her love has been the steadying and motivating factor that is and always has been present regardless of circumstances.

She believed in me when I did not even have a single clue about my own strength. She sent me to private school, struggled to pay my tuition all year, and never complained. Her attitude and belief in me forced me to keep working hard and improving.

Another incredible person is my wife, Shellie Diouf, whom I thank endlessly for her love and support. I spent lots of time at the library instead of being home or going out to see a movie together. While I was away from the house numerous times, researching, writing, and talking to other authors about the book, she was always supportive and motivating to keep me on my toes every day so that I could finish the book. I also want to extend thanks to my Dad, Niokhor, a great man. My siblings, Mahe, Ndof, Madou, Adja, Malick, Mareme, Khadim, Thillo, and special young children in my life, Fifi, Sophie, Mouhamed, and Lala, all for their love and support. My best friends, Mouhamadou Sylla, and Celina Henry, never stopped encouraging me. I also want to mention my father-in-law Joe who passed away but was a wonderful person, and I enjoyed spending time with him. My mother-in-law Barbara Callis, who has been a wonderful mother to me. Sister-in-law Annette and Brother-in-law Sylvester for their unconditional love.

Lastly, I thank the Garden City Library, where I spent most of my time reading and writing. The staff is friendly, welcoming, and very helpful. Thank you!

Made in United States
North Haven, CT
14 February 2023

32592975R00129